Managing Attention Deficit/Hyperactivity Disorder in the Inclusive Classroom

Practical Strategies
for Teachers

**John Alban-Metcalfe and
Juliette Alban-Metcalfe**

David Fulton Publishers

David Fulton Publishers Ltd
414 Chiswick High Road, London W4 5TF

www.fultonpublishers.co.uk

First published in Great Britain by David Fulton Publishers 2001
Reprinted 2002, 2003
10 9 8 7 6 5 4 3

British Library Cataloguing in Publication Data
A catalogue record for this book is available from the British Library.

ISBN 1–85346–749–9

Typeset by Book Production Services, London
Printed and bound by The Thanet Press, Margate.

Contents

Dedication

For Marjorie and Lou, wonderful parents and grandparents.

Royalties from the sale of this book will go to ADDISS, a registered charity
which disseminates information about AD/HD.

Acknowledgements

We would like to express our gratitude to Chris Johnson, Lynn Turner, Janet Dickenson, and Christine Congreve and colleagues, for valuable discussions about the practical implications of providing for children with AD/HD in mainstream schools. We would also like to thank Kath Stenton for drawing Figures 4.2 and 7.1, and Beverly Alimo-Metcalfe and Caroline Alban-Metcalfe, for their continuing love and support.

Preface

This book is designed to complement *Attention Deficit/Hyperactivity Disorder: A Practical Guide for Teachers* by Paul Cooper and Katherine Ideus, also published by David Fulton Publishers.

The book does not set out to provide recipes for instant success. Rather, it strives to offer the 'reflective practitioner' an up-to-date account of what is currently known about the nature and causes of AD/HD – which, it must be recognised, is an 'evolving concept', about the nature and educational and social implications of AD/HD, and about ways in which pupils with AD/HD can be educated effectively in 'inclusive' classrooms.

In so doing, we have examined the characteristics of 'inclusive' education, and analysed ways in which teachers can achieve the educational goals of: increasing academic attainment, developing interpersonal relations, and enhancing self-esteem. To illustrate how teachers can make optimal provision for pupils with AD/HD, we have included three case studies which illustrate the nature of difficulties encountered by such pupils, and ways in which teachers plan for and implement effective teaching strategies. Thus, chapters 5, 6 and 7 each start with a description of the characteristics of a child, and end with a critical evaluation of the educational provision made for that particular child. Certain details in the case studies have been changed, so that the child in question cannot be identified.

We have deliberately adopted a 'biopsychosocial' view of AD/HD, and a psycho-pedagogical perspective to analyse the way in which pupils learn and to devise appropriate intervention, since we consider this to be most readily applicable to understanding and implementing good classroom practice.

In most cases, the term 'child' has been used to refer to children and adolescents of pre-school or school age, except when there is reference to a specific sub-group, e.g. adolescents, as distinct from younger children.

Where more than one reference is relevant, the most recent published source is given, except when there is a large number of sources, in which cases, the reader is guided to a recent review of the relevant literature.

John Alban-Metcalfe and Juliette Alban-Metcalfe

March 2001

Notes on the contributors

John Alban-Metcalfe read Zoology at St Catherine's College, Oxford, and later obtained a PhD in Psychology. He has lectured and undertaken research in a number of European countries and in China, and has been a Visiting Professor (Catedrático) at the University of Santiago de Compostela. He is Head of Special Needs Education at Trinity and All Saints' University College, Leeds.

Juliette Alban-Metcalfe read Psychology at University of London Goldsmiths' College. She has worked as a University Research Assistant, and is currently a Project Consultant working in the National Health Service.

CHAPTER 1

Introduction

There is a high probability that among any class of 30 children, at least one child will show at least some of the symptoms of 'Attention-Deficit/Hyperactivity Disorder' (AD/HD). The characteristics or symptoms of AD/HD are a significant level of inattention, impulsiveness and hyperactivity. Each of these characteristics can have a profound effect on the personal development of the child, and the way in which s/he interacts with peers, siblings and adults. It is, however, the last of these characteristics that often leads children with AD/HD to be described as 'hyperactive', this being the aspect of their behaviour that causes them to be most difficult to manage at school as well as at home.

This book sets out to answer a number of questions that are commonly asked by parents and teachers. These questions include:

- What is AD/HD?
- What are its symptoms and causes?
- What is 'special' about the behaviour and attainment of children with AD/HD?
- What is 'inclusive' education and what does it mean in practice?
- How can provision best be made for identifying and assessing children with AD/HD, and teaching them in an 'inclusive' classroom?

What is AD/HD?

AD/HD is a condition, first described by an English physician, George Still, in 1902, to describe children (and adults) whose level of inattention, impulsiveness and/or hyperactive behaviour is such as to interfere with their daily functioning (e.g., Barkley, 1998). The extent to which the condition can affect the life of a child and her/his family can be great, as autobiographical accounts and accounts by parents of children with AD/HD record graphically (Fletcher, 1999; Frank, 1999).

Inattention shows itself in behaviours such as failing to give attention to detail, not listening to what is being said, difficulty with organising work and being easily distracted. *Hyperactivity* takes the form of behaviours such as fidgeting, leaving one's seat and running around excessively, while examples of *impulsiveness* (often referred to as *impulsivity*) are blurting out answers before questions are finished, difficulty in waiting or taking turns. The fourth edition of the *Diagnostic and Statistical Manual – 4 (DSM-IV-TR)*, produced by the American Psychiatric Association (2000) gives two scales for diagnosing AD/HD: a scale for assessing inattention, comprising nine criteria; and a scale for assessing hyperactivity-impulsivity, comprising six hyperactivity criteria and three impulsivity criteria (Table 1.1). There is much overlap between AD/HD and 'Hyperkinetic Disorder', as defined by the World Health Organisation (WHO) in the *International Classification of Diseases – 10* (WHO, 1990) (Table 1.2).

However, the exact nature of AD/HD is not yet known, and it is best regarded as an 'evolving concept' (BPS, 1996).

Sub-types of AD/HD

The diagnosis of AD/HD Combined type depends on the presence to a significant degree of six of the nine criteria for inattention, *plus* six of the nine criteria for hyperactivity-impulsiveness. It also requires evidence, (a) that some of the inattentive or hyperactive-impulsive symptoms presented themselves before seven years of age, (b) that some of the symptoms manifest themselves in at least two different settings (e.g., home and school), (c) that the symptoms result in significant impairment in academic, occupational or social situations, and (d) that the symptoms cannot more readily be accounted for by another psychological or psychiatric condition.

Some children show six or more of the characteristics of *either* inattention, *or* hyperactivity-impulsiveness, but *not* both. Such children are sometimes described as having 'AD/HD Inattentive-type', or 'AD/HD Hyperactive-impulsive-type', respectively (Barkley, 1998).

It may, however, be the case that AD/HD Inattentive-type is a separate condition. In support of this suggestion is evidence, (i) that a different kind of attention is involved in AD/HD Inattentive-type, and (ii) that such children have greater difficulty with memory and with perceptual-motor speed than their Hyperactive-impulsive counterparts. Inattentive-type children are also described by their teachers and parents as cognitively slower, more prone to daydreaming and more socially withdrawn. The inclusion of a slash between the letters AD/HD is to indicate that some children suffer only from having attention difficulties, others from only hyperactivity and impulsiveness, and others from both kinds of problem.

Table 1.1: Criteria for Attention Deficit/Hyperactivity Disorder

A.1. Inattention: At least six of the following symptoms of innattention have persisted for at least 6 months to a degree that is maladaptive and inconsistent with development level.

    a.   Often fails to give close attention to details or makes careless mistakes in schoolwork, work, or other activities.

    b.   Often has difficulty sustaining attention in tasks or play activities.

    c.   Often does not seem to listen when spoken to directly.

    d.   Often does not follow through on instructions and fails to finish schoolwork, chores or duties in the workplace (not due to oppositional behaviour or failure to understand instructions).

    e.   Often has difficulties organising tasks and activities.

    f.   Often avoids, dislikes or is reluctant to engage in tasks that require sustained effort (such as schoolwork or homework).

    g.   Often loses things necessary for tasks or activities (e.g., toys, school assignments, pencils, books or tools).

    h.   Is often easily distracted by extraneous stimuli.

    i.   Is often forgetful in daily activities.

A.2. Hyperactivity-Impulsivity. At least six of the following symptoms of hyperactivity-impulsivity have persisted for at least 6 months to a degree that is maladaptive and inconsistent with development level:

Hyperactivity

    a.   Often fidgets with hands or feet and squirms in seat.

    b.   Often leaves seat in classroom or in other situations in which remaining seated is expected.

    c.   Often runs about or climbs excessively in situations where it is inappropriate (in adolescents or adults, may be limited to subjective feelings of restlessness).

    d.   Often has difficulty playing or engaging in leisure activities quietly.

    e.   Is always 'on the go' and acts as if 'driven by a motor'.

    f.   Often talks excessively.

Impulsivity

    g.   Often blurts out answers to questions before they have been completed.

    h.   Often has difficulty awaiting turn.

    i.   Often interrupts or intrudes on others (e.g., butts into conversations or games).

B.   Some symptoms that cause impairment were present before age 7.

C.   Some symptoms that cause impairment must be present in two or more settings (e.g., at school, work, and at home)

D.   There must be clear evidence of clinically significant impairment in social, academic or occupational functioning.

E.   Does not occur exclusively during the course of a Pervasive Developmental Disorder, Schizophrenia or other Psychotic Disorder, or a Personality Disorder.

Based on Diagnostic and Statistical Manual of Mental Disorders (DSM-IV-TR) (2000). Washington DC. American Psychiatric Association.

Table 1.2: Hyperkinetic Syndrome

A.	**Demonstrate abnormality of attention and activity at home, for the age and developmental level of the child, as evidenced by at least three of the following attention problems:**

    1.   Short duration to spontaneous activities.
    2.   Often leaving play activities unfinished.
    3.   Overfrequent changes between activities.
    4.   Undue lack of persistence at tasks set by adults.
    5.   Unduly high distractibility during study, (e.g., homework or reading assignment);
        and by at least two of the following:
    6.   Continuous motor restlessness (running, jumping, etc).
    7.   Markedly excessive fidgeting or wriggling during spontaneous activities.
    8.   Markedly excessive activity in situations expecting relative stillness (e.g., mealtimes, travel, visiting church).
    9.   Difficulty in remaining seated when required.

B.   Demonstrate abnormality of attention and activity at school or nursery (if applicable), for the age and development level of the child, as evidenced by at least two of the following attention problems:
    1.   Undue lack of persistence at tasks.
    2.   Unduly high distractibility, i.e., often orienting towards extrinsic stimuli.
    3.   Overfrequent changes between activities when choice is allowed.
    4.   Excessively short duration of play activities,
        and by at least two of the following activity problems:
    5.   Continuous and excessive motor restlessness (running, jumping, etc.) in school.
    6.   Markedly excessive fidgeting and wriggling in structured situation.
    7.   Excessive levels of off-task activity during tasks.
    8.   Unduly often out of seat when required to be sitting.

C.   Directly observed abnormality of attention or activity. This must be excessive for the child's age and development level. The evidence may be any of the following:
    1.   Direct observation of the criteria in A or B above, i.e., not solely the report of parent and/or teacher.
    2.   Observation of abnormal levels of motor activity, or off-task behaviour, or lack of persistence in activities, in a setting outside home or school (e.g., clinic or laboratory).
    3.   Significant impairment of performance on psychometric test of attention.

D.   Does not meet criteria for pervasive developmental disorder, mania, depressive or anxiety disorder.

E.   Onset before the age of six years.

F.   Duration of at least six months.

G.   IQ above 50.

The research diagnosis of Hyperkinetic disorder requires the definite presence of abnormal levels of inattention and restlessness that are pervasive across situations and persistent over time, that can be demonstrated by direct observation, and that are not caused by other disorders such as autism or affective disorders.

Eventually, assessment instruments should develop to the point where it is possible to take a quantitative cut-off score on reliable, valid, and standardised measures of hyperactive behaviour in the home and classroom, corresponding to the 95th percentile on both measures. Such criteria would then replace A and B above.

From the *International Classification of Diseases* (10th ed.) by the World Health Organization, 1990, Geneva.

Incidence

The estimated prevalence of all AD/HD among children of school age in England and Wales is around 5 per cent, not all of whom are diagnosed, with the stricter criteria for Hyperkinetic Disorder being met in around 1 per cent of cases (NICE, 2000). It is generally agreed that the condition is much more common in boys than in girls (estimates vary from a ratios of 6:1 to 3:1). However, since AD/HD is not an 'all-or-nothing' condition, many more children than those diagnosed as meeting six out of nine criteria may have many of the symptoms to such a degree as to interfere with their schoolwork and their relationships with others, but not be classed as having AD/HD. It is, therefore, best to regard AD/HD as existing along a continuum. By no means all children diagnosed as having AD/HD have a Statement of Special Educational Needs (SEN).

What is 'inclusive education'?

The term 'educational inclusion' was coined to replace the term 'educational integration', or 'functional integration' (DES, 1978), which fell into disrepute. As Farrell (2000) points out, 'the aim [of inclusive education] is to encourage schools to reconsider teaching approaches, pupil groupings and use of support so that they respond to the needs of all pupils' (p. 77). He goes on to note that inclusion differs from integration in that, in the latter, the assumption is that the school system will remain the same, but that *additional* arrangements will be made for pupils with special educational needs (SEN). Whether inclusive education, as practised in most European countries, goes far enough in meeting the educational and social needs of pupils with SEN has been questioned by Molina y Garcia and Alban-Metcalfe (1998). They argue that for education to be truly inclusive, school curricula should set out to address the particular needs of pupils with SEN, and not a combination of the needs of the majority of pupils plus various economic factors, with pupils with SEN being a kind of 'bolt-on' group (cf. Mittler, 2000).

The arguments for and against inclusion have been reviewed recently by Letch (2000). In essence, they are based on:

(a) principles – the right of all children, irrespective of the nature and degree of any 'special need', to be educated along with their peers in mainstream schools, *versus* the right of children with certain kinds of 'special need' not to be disadvantaged by being denied specialist, segregated provision; and

(b) practice – whether it is possible to provide inclusive education without the presence of certain children having deleterious effects on the learning of other children in the class or school.

The issue is hotly argued in the case of children who have emotional and behavioural difficulties (EBD), a category which includes children with AD/HD. Thus, for example, the General Secretary of the NAS/UWT suggested that the inclusion of children with EBD could be a 'big problem', an 'absolute disaster' and bring 'untold misery' (quoted in Farrell, 1998). Conversely, the government is committed to a policy of social inclusion, and has offered help and guidance to enable schools to reduce exclusions (DfEE, 1999), and the characteristics of schools that are effective in achieving educational and social inclusion have been identified (OFSTED, 1999; Richards, 1999).

The view expressed here is that, for children with AD/HD, as for other children with EBD, educational inclusion is a moral imperative, and thus a goal that we must vigorously strive to achieve.

CHAPTER 2

The behaviour of children with AD/HD

What are the causes of AD/HD?

Several explanations have been put forward to account for the symptoms of AD/HD. Cognitive research has sought to account for impulsive and hyperactive behaviour in terms of, (a) some kind of neuropsychological processing dysfunction affecting the 'inhibition control system', and/or (b) temporal processing systems, which act generally or are situation specific, and/or (c) 'energic' or 'state' mechanisms, hypothesised to influence speed and accuracy of responses to sensory stimuli. Impairment in speed of information processing and ability to focus or select an object for attention is seen as the cause of the symptoms of inattention (Cooper, 1999; Tannock, 1998).

Behaviour Inhibition System

The cognitive theory proposed by Barkley (1997, 1998) has implications for educational practice. This suggests that children with AD/HD behave as they do because they have great difficulty in controlling their behaviour, owing to a malfunction of their 'behaviour inhibition system' (BIS). Thus, in tasks requiring sustained attention, failure of the BIS leads the child to lack the motivation to stay on task, and thus to jump from one task to another. Similarly, difficulty with self-control causes them to be unable to control bodily movements, as in fidgeting or walking around the classroom, or to act on impulse, as in difficulty with turn taking, or blurting out answers. Also, different 'executive functions' of the BIS — working memory (verbal and non-verbal), and analysis and synthesis of ideas and actions, all of which are necessary for hindsight and foresight; self-regulation of arousal, emotions and motivation — may function/malfunction to a greater or lesser extent, and thus affect academic work and ability to deal with interpersonal situations.

Although the BIS model is unproved, it is consistent with everyday observations that children with AD/HD, (a) *can* attend over very long periods of time to tasks that they find interesting, and (b) *will* attend to tasks, provided that their behaviour is closely supervised. Thus, in activities as different as playing video games or watching television, and fishing, the motivation for sustained attention would appear to be intrinsic interest in the task. Also, 'social motivation', i.e., motivation attributable to someone else's interest in what they are doing, is a key variable.

AD/HD as a 'biopsychosocial' phenomenon

All such theories fail, however, to present a complete picture. This is because they do not take into account the effect of psychological and social factors, which include the way that individuals with AD/HD perceive themselves, the way that they are perceived and treated by others and the way in which their behaviour is consonant or at variance with societal norms and values. Thus, AD/HD is best understood as resulting from a complex interplay of biological, psychological and social factors, i.e., a 'biopsychosocial' phenomenon (Cooper, 1999).

It is not, therefore, valid to regard AD/HD as an exclusively 'within-child' characteristic – the symptoms of AD/HD are the result of interaction between the child and her/his environment. This environment comprises individual and collective actions of other individuals (family and friends, professionals and the public), and cultural norms and expectations. The implications include that certain aspects of school life can cause, or at least contribute to, the symptoms of AD/HD, thus:

1. a multi-agency approach should be adopted in the assessment of, and provision for, children with AD/HD; and
2. such provision can only be made as the result of changes both within the child *and* within the school and wider society.

Heritability

There is evidence that AD/HD is a genetically based condition, which means that it can be inherited, though the extent to which the condition shows itself varies from one generation to another – sometimes a parent may show the condition more severely than the child, or *vice versa*. This is not, however, to deny that environmental factors affect the extent to which the symptoms are manifested in a given child. Parents and teachers can play a key role in helping the child to learn how to interact more effectively with the world. Conversely, it is important to remember that AD/HD is *not* caused by bad parenting, *nor* by bad teaching; what parents and teachers can do is to help the child to develop strategies for coping with her/his condition.

Diet

There is also evidence that, among some children, diet can cause or contribute to the symptoms of AD/HD (Kinder, 1999).

Age

There are age-related differences in the symptoms, such that, while inattention persists throughout life, hyperactivity tends to decrease among adolescents and adults. Also, the three impulsivity criteria fail to reflect high-risk adolescent and adult behaviours associated with AD/HD in the areas of sexuality, substance abuse, and driving.

Gender

Although the same diagnostic criteria are applied to boys and girls, it must be recognised that the symptoms of AD/HD and the associated behaviours are different in men and women. Furthermore, girls are more likely to have Inattentive-type than Combined-type AD/HD.

What is 'special' about the behaviour and attainment of children with AD/HD?

The answer to this question comes in three parts: (1) those behaviours that are always associated with AD/HD, i.e., the symptoms or 'morbidity' of the condition; (2) those characteristics and behaviours, which are often found among children with AD/HD; and (3) those psychological or psychiatric disorders, referred to as 'co-morbid' disorders, which are often associated with the condition.

1. Behaviour of children with AD/HD – inattention, hyperactivity, impulsiveness

The characteristics or 'morbidity' of AD/HD has been defined in terms of the 18 criteria (Table 1.1), nine of which refer to different aspects of inattention, and the remaining nine to hyperactivity (six items) and impulsivity (three items) (APA, 2000; Cooper and Ideus, 1996; Robin, 1998). However, Brown (1995) made the suggestion, for which Alban-Metcalfe (1999) found some empirical support, that only five of the inattention items actually relate to attention, with the remaining four relating to different aspects of cognitive functioning, such as organisation.

Inattention

Attention is measured in two ways – focused attention, as in tasks that require a child to point to a particular letter or shape, and sustained attention, in which the child is required to attend to the same task over an extended period of time. Children with AD/HD only have difficulty with the latter, not with the former. Thus, they turn their attention to each new stimulus as it presents itself and as a consequence have difficulty in completing tasks.

Auditory distractions include another child tapping their pencil, a sound which most children will hear, but then ignore; visually distracting stimuli may include the pattern on a rug – to which the child then gives full attention – or objects on the desk or anywhere in the classroom. Since almost all school learning requires sustained concentration on tasks, being easily distractible is a significant disability.

However, what at first seems paradoxical is that children with AD/HD will spend many hours watching television, playing with their computer, building models, tending animals or even fishing. When they are active in this way, they appear to be able to apply a kind of 'filter', which blocks out any irrelevant stimuli. Some parents and teachers often comment that they appear to be in a kind of 'trance', such that, in order to gain their attention, they have to place themselves physically between the child and the stimulus, for example, standing in front of the television.

Some children say that they can only do their homework to the accompaniment of loud music, and that in its absence, they tend to hear and be distracted by every sound, however small. On the other hand, other children appear to experience 'sensory overload' caused, for example, by the noise and bustle in a shopping mall, or at a children's party. In such cases, the 'overload' may be attributable to their inability to block out external stimuli. Experiencing difficulties of this kind can be a great cause of distress to a child, and become a barrier to partaking fully in a normal social life.

The other symptoms of inattention involve difficulties with organisation of tasks, avoidance of mental effort, losing things and being forgetful. Here, the common theme seems to be ability to organise – to organise tasks, to organise ideas, to organise things so that one knows where they are, to organise one's thoughts so that one can remember appointments, tasks that have to be completed, etc.

The importance of the organisational aspect of AD/HD is twofold: the organisational/planning functions of the brain control, (i) attentiveness *versus* inattention; and (ii) the *way* in which we process information.

Impulsiveness

Impulsiveness shows itself in three ways. Behaviourally, the child wants to have things immediately, does whatever comes to mind, opting for short-term pleasure despite long-term pain, and generally does not consider the effects of own actions. This makes conformity to rules and regulations difficult. In academic contexts, s/he blurts out answers to questions and tends to rush through schoolwork which, in combination with inattention, leads to overlooking important details and making careless mistakes. Emotionally, the child becomes frustrated easily, and will respond by becoming a victim and/or being moody, and/or being agitated and physically or verbally aggressive. Aggression may be directed at others or at self (e.g., suicidal behaviour).

Hyperactivity

This also shows itself in three main ways. One, is continuous bodily movements, e.g., fidgeting, squirming in a seat. The second, is a feeling of being confined when in the classroom for a long period of time, or when having to sit at a desk and study for a long time. Third, is over-activity, which may take the form of non-stop talking (especially in girls), continually badgering the teacher, and/or being 'on the go' all the time, day and night. The child may only need four or five hours sleep at night. A small minority of adolescents in which hyperactivity persists, feel that they would go crazy if they did not have something to do.

2. Behaviour and attainment associated with AD/HD

Children with AD/HD often show other characteristics or behaviours that are associated with the condition (Barkley, 1998; Cooper and Ideus, 1996; Pliszka, *et al.*, 1999; Robin, 1998; Teeter, 1998). While these are a cause for concern, they can also serve to guide intervention by teachers and parents. In some cases, it is easy to understand how and why these characteristics or behaviours might develop; in other cases, it is not so evident.

Intellectual development

It has been reported that children with AD/HD score 7–15 points behind peers on IQ tests. However, whether this is a genuine phenomenon, or a test-related artefact, such that they score poorly because of inattentive and/or impulsive response style, is not clear; also, in some studies, the samples were ill-defined. Conversely, there are theoretical reasons for expecting that children with AD/HD are likely to represent the entire spectrum of intellectual development, from 'gifted/more able' to those with severe learning difficulties. At the same time, a small but significant negative correlation between the severity of the condition and verbal IQ might be expected because verbal IQ depends on working memory and internalised speech, two areas in which children with AD/HD have difficulties. In most cases, children with AD/HD are of average to high intelligence.

Academic performance

A learning difficulty may be defined as a significant discrepancy between a child's general mental abilities or 'intelligence', and their achievement in schoolwork. Among children with AD/HD, such difficulties are evident in literacy, numeracy, and other subjects that require sustained mental effort, particularly when the tasks do not hold any natural or intrinsic interest for the child.

Adaptive functioning

This term refers to 'lower-order' age-appropriate skills, such as self-help skills required in fastening/unfastening buttons, eating and drinking without help. Here, children with AD/HD tend to function at the lower-average/borderline range, in spite of having a normal IQ. The greater the IQ adaptive functioning discrepancy, the greater the level of AD/HD impairment and the more likely the possibility of co-morbid psychiatric disorder and substance abuse.

Speech and language development

The evidence of a link between AD/HD and delay in the onset of talking in early childhood is inconsistent. At the same time, there is evidence that children with AD/HD are more likely to have problems with expressive language than with receptive language. This link was not found among children who only had higher than normal levels of inattentiveness (AD/HD – Inattention type). Such children did, however, experience more difficulty with the organisation of their expressive language and with conversational pragmatics (i.e., conventional meanings of words and expressions), than either 'normal' children or children diagnosed as having learning difficulties.

Children with AD/HD are likely to talk more than other children. However, with tasks that involve organising and generating speech in response to specific demands, they tended to talk less, or to be dysfluent. Thus, their difficulties would appear to be not so much with speech and language as such, but rather with organising and monitoring their thinking – in other words with their 'executive processing'.

Internalisation of language

There is evidence to suggest that, among all children, 'external private speech', that is, speech uttered out loud by children but addressed to themselves, or to no one in particular, is important in the self-regulation of behaviour (as also in adults) when solving problems (Vygotsky, 1978). Also, that as the child matures, external private speech develops into 'inner private speech', leading, in turn, to wholly internalised verbal thought. Children with AD/HD, however, are less mature in their self-speech and seem to be developmentally delayed in this process. Thus, children with difficulties with sustained attention tend to use more external private speech and less inner speech than 'normal' children. However, among children with AD/HD, as with other children, the amount of external private speech is associated with task-relevant behaviour – the more difficult or more complex the task, the more the external private speech. The use of private speech is one of the strategies that learners use with tasks of this kind, a strategy that children with AD/HD need to be taught. It has also been suggested that delayed internalisation of language may, at least in part, be a cause of difficulties with rule-government behaviour.

Memory, organisation and planning

Children with AD/HD are just as capable as other children in the long-term storage and retrieval of information, but appear to have difficulties in using their 'working memory'. Working memory is the capacity to hold information in mind over a short period of time, and is used to help a child with sustained attention to tasks, to enable thinking processes to take place, and to guide and inform her/him about the effectiveness of their actions and responses.

One way of thinking about working memory is in terms of two systems. These are: non-verbal working memory, concerned with remembering shapes and imitating the actions of others; and verbal working memory, involved in tasks that range from retention and repetition of words and numbers, through carrying out arithmetical calculations, to tasks involving organisation and planning, as in problem solving or planning a work schedule. Effective functioning in all these areas is clearly relevant to successful performance in academic and social contexts.

Children with AD/HD appear to have difficulty with imitating lengthy and novel sequences of body movements. Difficulties with activities involving mental computation, digit span (particularly backwards) and coding tasks; tasks involving the storage of large amounts of complex verbal information (but not simple verbal information); the development of strategies for organising material to be remembered, have also been reported among children and adults with AD/HD.

Another way of thinking about working memory is in terms of functions. One of these is its retrospective function, or hindsight; the other is its prospective function, or foresight. Research suggests that children with AD/HD are deficient in hindsight, which means that they have difficulty in altering subsequent actions in the light of immediately past mistakes. In relation to forethought, these children often fail to use stimuli warning that a response is required, with their success rate falling off more steeply than 'normal' children as the preparatory interval is increased.

Evidence of the difficulty encountered by children with AD/HD in planning comes from their poor performance in problem-solving tasks, such as 'Tower of London' and 'Tower of Hanoi'. These tasks, which require the child to construct a design using coloured disks and upright pegs, subject to certain constraints, rely heavily on working memory (verbal and non-verbal). They also require forethought and planning, involving the ability to represent mentally and test out ways of removing and replacing the disks, so as to match a pre-specified design. There is inconsistent evidence that they also have difficulty with mazes. The implications for having a poor working memory are, therefore, not limited simply to 'memory activities' but have a fundamental effect on the child's ability to benefit from the use of hindsight and forethought, and in planning. The implications are equally evident in social as in academic contexts.

Rule-governed behaviour

Rules, whether they are imposed by the parents or the teacher, can be thought of as ways of controlling or channelling behaviour so as to achieve long-term goals. It is undoubtedly the case that children with AD/HD have difficulty with tasks in which the following of rules is a pre-requisite for success[1]. It has been found that children with AD/HD perform better under conditions of immediate, rather than delayed, reward. Also, they experience great difficulty when performing tasks in which delays are imposed within the task, when such delays increase in duration, and with tasks in which unrelated consequences occur within the tasks. Furthermore, they encounter difficulty with tasks which have delayed or long-term rewards, rather than where the reward is immediate.

Is has also been suggested that they have a greater and more rapid decline in performance, compared to other children, when their rewards move from being continuous to intermittent. However, the evidence for this is inconsistent and the effectiveness of different patterns of reinforcement appears, not surprisingly, to be related to the difficulty of the task. Thus, difficult tasks require continuous reinforcement, easier ones do not. Also, the length of the delay between completing a task and receiving some form of reinforcement may be an important variable in maintaining a high level of performance.

The suggestion is, therefore, that it is close adherence to rules that leads to successful performance on tasks. On the other hand, it has also been suggested that these findings may be better explained in terms of poor self-regulation of motivational state. In other words, that the effect of continual teacher (or parental) intervention is to maintain the child's level of motivation. The motivational interpretation is consistent with the suggestion that children with AD/HD have more difficulty with tasks that are imposed on them when they have to carry them out on their own, than when an adult is directly supervising them. The child's difficulties seem to stem not so much from *knowing what to do*, as from *doing what they know*.

Attempts have been made to explain seemingly conflicting observations in terms of differences in the working memory and internalised language of 'normal' children, compared to those with AD/HD. Better developed working memories and more internalised language, in association with more rule-governed behaviour, are interpreted as leading to a capacity to bridge temporal delays between reinforcements. The behaviour of children with AD/HD is controlled more by immediate and external sources of reward.

Sense of time

Studies of sense of time tend to suggest that children with AD/HD are less able than other children to estimate length of time accurately, possibly as a consequence of their poor inhibition and difficulties with working memory. Such children also appear to perform poorly on tasks in which temporal delays are imposed, and in which there are uncertainties about timing.

Regulation of emotion, motivation and arousal

Since the earliest study by Still in 1902, irritability, hostility, excitability and general hyper-responsiveness toward others have been reported in the literature. However, although children with AD/HD appear to have difficulties with emotional self-control, a link between AD/HD and poor emotional self-regulation has not been confirmed. Children with AD/HD do not, however, have any difficulty in recognising the emotions of others.

Two other commonly described attributes of AD/HD are poor motivation and impaired persistence on tasks, particularly on tasks that involve repetitive responding, with little or no reinforcement. Reports of lower levels of persistence of children with AD/HD, on activities that include productivity in arithmetic tasks and on laboratory tasks, have been interpreted as evidence of difficulties in their self-regulation of motivation. The evidence is not, however, straightforward. Thus, it seems that on tasks accompanied by immediate and continuous rewards, children with AD/HD do not differ from 'normal' children. When the reinforcement is partial, some studies reported a relative decline in performance among the former, while other studies did not. Important modulating effects would appear to be task duration and difficulty, and perhaps also the tediousness of the task.

Neurophysiological and psychological evidence leads to the conclusion that children with AD/HD show greater variability in the extent to which their brains are aroused and thus activated (though there appear to be differences between girls and boys). In other words, their brains, or at least the frontal regions, appear to be under-stimulated.

Sensory-motor development and physical health

Although they do not have difficulties with their peripheral hearing, there is evidence that suggests that children with AD/HD are hyper-sensitive to auditory loudness. Also, research suggests that they have difficulty with the accurate discrimination of speech. The implication is the need for teachers and parents to reduce background noise when talking to or teaching the child. Some children with AD/HD find it extremely difficult to work in a noisy primary classroom.

In terms of physical functioning, there is inconsistent evidence of an association between AD/HD and visual impairment. Also, evidence of links between AD/HD and enuresis or encopresis is inconsistent, though there is consistent evidence of reduced sleep. Children with AD/HD are more likely than other children to experience accidental injuries, with as many as 57 per cent being described as 'accident-prone', and up to 15 per cent having had four or more serious accidental injuries. It may be, however, that some of these injuries are attributable to aggressive or oppositional behaviour, which is often associated with AD/HD.

Links have also been reported between accidents among children as pedestrians or cyclists and performance on tests of vigilance and impulse control, and ratings of being hyperactive-aggressive. Other relationships with AD/HD include increased likelihood of speeding and car accidents, crime, suicide attempts, substance abuse and risk-taking behaviour in general.

Again, there is conflicting evidence of greater risk of delays in crawling, walking or general motor development, though as a group, children with AD/HD commonly have poor motor coordination. It has been suggested that this may be owing to a 'motor-control deficit'. Such a deficit is thought not to show itself at an attentional or information-processing stage, but to be associated rather with decision making and the organisation of responses.

Handwriting, which comprises the complex sequencing of simpler motor movements, has been reported as being less mature in children with AD/HD, and to be significantly impaired among those with Combined and Inattentive sub-type, especially the former.

Creativity, flexibility and perseveration.

It has been suggested that creativity, as measured by flexibility and originality of ideas, may be impaired in children with AD/HD. Such evidence is consistent with observations of below normal creativity during free play and on non-verbal creativity tasks, among children with an average level of intelligence. It is also consonant with evidence that, when presented with problem-solving situations and contexts that require thoughtful formulation of novel responses, children with AD/HD often offer over-learned and automatic responses.

Also, children with AD/HD tend to show perseverative behaviour on card-sorting tasks by being able to use existing rules, but unable to change this behaviour when new rules come into operation. This behaviour may, however, be best interpreted as suggesting not that they are unable to formulate new rules, but that they are unable to adhere to them.

However, the conclusions about creativity appear to be based on the false assumption that creativity is the same thing as 'divergent thinking' (which is measured only in terms of flexibility and originality in thinking). They are also at variance with the observations of parents, teachers and others that children with AD/HD can be extremely inventive in the kind of activities they get up to (e.g., Fletcher, 1999).

3. Disorders associated with AD/HD

In addition to the attainment and behaviour commonly associated with AD/HD, children with AD/HD may also have one or more of a small number of other, different disorders, referred to as 'co-morbid' conditions or the 'co-morbidity' (e.g., Barkley, 1998; Cooper and Ideus, 1996; Pliszka, *et al.*, 1999; Robin, 1998).

These include: anxiety and mood disorders; oppositional defiant disorder; conduct disorder. Although each of these is thought to have distinct diagnostic criteria, some of the criteria overlap those for AD/HD, so it is sometimes difficult to make a definitive diagnostic distinction between them. In a study of Canadian children, it was estimated that up to 44 per cent of children with AD/HD may also have at least one other psychiatric condition, with 32 per cent having two such disorders and 11 per cent having three.

Anxiety and mood disorders

It has been estimated that up to 30 per cent of children and adolescents with AD/HD also have an anxiety or neurotic disorder. One of these, Bipolar Disorder or 'manic depression', which is characterised by swings of mood lasting over a period of weeks or months, has also commonly been reported among children with AD/HD, with estimated frequencies as high as 20 per cent. These figures must, however, be interpreted with extreme caution, since there is considerable overlap between the *DSM-IV-TR* criteria for the two conditions; a more realistic overlap may be 6 per cent.

Oppositional Defiant Disorder

This is a disorder that is characterised by persistently more defiant and argumentative behaviour in opposition typically to adult authority figures, and a more negative, hostile and angry disposition, than is typical for a child of the same age. There is consistent evidence of a correlation between hyperactivity and aggression, and it has been estimated that up to 40 per cent of children with AD/HD and up to 65 per cent of teenagers also show signs of Oppositional Defiant Disorder.

Conduct Disorder

Conduct Disorder (CD) constitutes a persistent pattern of behaviour that violates the basic rights of others, or important societal rules and norms. Examples of such behaviour include aggressive behaviour that threatens physical harm to people or animals, destruction of property, theft or deceit. Up to 60 per cent of adolescents with AD/HD show more serious forms of CD, such as stealing, physical aggression and truancy; and there is a strong link between AD/HD and substance abuse.

Conclusion

What the evidence suggests is that the following conclusions can be drawn:

1. that children with AD/HD experience difficulties which are a direct consequence of the way in which they process information – some aspects of their processing of information do not function efficiently. For example, a deficit in working memory makes it difficult for a child to do addition or take-away sums when lots of numbers are involved;

2. that some of these information-processing difficulties are more far reaching in their effect. For example, deficits in using foresight and hindsight, particularly when coupled with a working memory deficit, make it difficult for a child to organise and plan academic tasks. Deficits of this kind cause difficulty in social situations, owing to an inability to predict accurately how others will act;

3. that – by way of contrast – some children with AD/HD do show very high levels of competence on tasks that require a high level of skill, such as model making, caring for a pet animal, and information-processing skills, such as those involved in using a computer;

4. that children with AD/HD experience difficulty in controlling their behaviour, which shows itself both in difficulty with remaining on-task and in achieving rule-governed behaviour;

5. that some of the difficulty in controlling own behaviour manifests itself in lack of motivation to do certain tasks, notably those which hold no intrinsic interest to the child;

6. that – again by way of contrast – children with AD/HD are commonly reported to be highly motivated to remain on-task, even to the point of excessive perseveration, when engaged in activities of their own choosing;

7. That they are likely to have very low self-esteem.

Some of the difficulties that children with AD/HD experience with academic tasks are, therefore, a direct consequence of deficits in their information-processing capacities, while others are motivational in original. In other words, sometimes they do not achieve because they are unable, but sometimes they do not achieve because they do not wish to try – sometimes it's can't do; sometimes it's could do but don't want to.

All this paints a picture that is much more than of a child who is simply difficult to deal with at home and in class. There is no question that children with AD/HD can, in some cases, be extremely difficult to handle. However, while the reasons for their patterns of behaviour are deep-seated, they also offer clues as to how provision can best be made.

Note

1. It has been suggested that difficulty in adhering to rules and instructions may be a primary condition of, or at least a condition associated with, AD/HD (e.g., APA, 2000).

CHAPTER 3

The inclusive classroom

What is an 'inclusive' classroom?

An inclusive classroom is one in which continuing emphasis on valuing individual differences leads *all* pupils, irrespective of social or cultural background, disability or difficulty in learning, to succeed in terms of the fulfilment of academic and social goals, and in the development of positive attitudes to self and others.

How can 'inclusion' be achieved in practice?

Inclusive education can only be achieved by schools that: (a) are committed to maximising inclusion and minimising exclusion; (b) plan for diversity; and (c) work towards developing appropriate environments for all children, rather than attempting to oblige all pupils to 'fit the school' (Ainscow, 1997; DfEE, 1999; Richards, 1999). The various factors that can contribute to the development of an inclusive classroom are summarised in Figure 3.1, though it must be recognised that inclusion can only be achieved if they interact with one another in a positive, harmonious way.

Purposeful and sensitive leadership

The essential attribute of successful leaders is the capacity to transform their organisation or department, so as to achieve desired goals in a way that ensures the commitment and cooperation of all staff. In order to achieve this, leaders at all levels need to have a clear vision of what is desired and strategies to achieve the vision, and the ability to inspire and to empower staff in such a way that they wish to contribute, together with the ability to manage resources effectively (Alimo-Metcalfe and Alban-Metcalfe, 2001). The most effective schools are characterised by leadership of this kind, in which leaders at all levels

Purposeful and sensitive leadership			School ethos	
Academic standards	Interpersonal relations	Standards of attendance and behaviour	Pupil self-esteem	Pupil attitudes to school
Curriculum content and organisation				Home-school links
Quality of teaching		*Inclusive Education*		School-community links
Quality of resources				Multi-agency cooperation
Access to latest research	In-service education and training		Attitudes of staff	Teacher self-esteem

Figure 3.1: Factors affecting inclusive education

in the school show a strong commitment to the school, to its staff and to all the pupils in the school. This kind of leadership is effective in changing attitudes among staff and pupils and in developing a sense of confidence throughout the school (OFSTED, 2000). It also leads to changes in each of the other factors identified as contributing to educational inclusion.

School ethos

The ethos of a school is, by definition, its principal characteristic, and comprises the attitudes, intentions and actions of all the individuals who make up the school community – the teaching and learning support staff, the non-teaching staff and parent helpers, school governors and the pupils (Lorenz, 2001). It affects not only those who work in the school on a regular basis, but also those who have occasional contact with the school. What a school is trying to achieve in terms of its ethos is often defined in the Mission Statement, and is an attribute which pervades all aspects of school life.

At a minimum, a school's ethos can be judged by questions such as:

- whether any group of pupils has a 'hard time';
- whether there is bullying or name calling, or differential treatment for boys and girls,

pupils with special needs or pupils from different family or ethnic backgrounds;

- whether all pupils are treated fairly during lessons and generally at school;
- whether pupils have high self-esteem, and know where to go for personal support (OFSTED, undated).

At best, it should be judged in terms of:

- whether the headteacher and all staff show strongly positive attitudes to all pupils and are active in meeting their emotional as well as educational needs;
- whether they strive, through differentiation of the curriculum, teaching methods and resources and in fostering strong and effective home-school, school-community and multi-agency support, to enable all pupils to achieve their educational and social poten-tial;
- whether the school is effective in promoting spiritual, moral and social values.

Pupils with EBD benefit from adult-pupil relationships which are supportive, non-judgemental and non-threatening; and identify a need for adults who are keen to adopt a pastoral role (DfEE, 1999; Richards, 1999).

Pupil attitudes to school and to each other; standards of behaviour

Pupil attitudes can be considered in relation to two groups of pupils – the 'givers' and the 'receivers' of help. Both benefit from being given worthwhile, but challenging tasks to do, coupled with fulsome recognition of their achievements. The 'givers' tend to comprise older and/or more able pupils, who can help the younger and/or less able, for example, through paired learning activities and through the establishment of 'buddy' systems, leading to greater social inclusion. The 'receivers' gain by becoming more competent academically and socially, by having their achievements recognised and by thus becoming more self-confident.

Schools' efforts can be judged in terms of pupil support, guidance and welfare, and in provision for pupils' social, moral, cultural and spiritual development. Where schools are successful, this is the result of promoting 'a positive approach to attainment and progress ... hand in hand with a positive approach to behaviour, attitudes and personal development' (OFSTED, 2000: 24); both approaches should be followed simultaneously, rather than sequentially.

In schools where inclusion is successful, good behaviour is based on:

- good classroom work, with clearly established links between the following: high teacher expectations and challenging targets; effective teacher support so that pupils can achieve success; positive responses from the pupils; monitoring and support of pupil progress; rewarding of pupil success, coupled with:

- good discipline, which is promoted through: clear policies, which are understood by all; reinforcement of responsible behaviour; emphasis on self-discipline and respect for others; well-planned, graduated sanctions applied fairly and sensitively; consistency on the part of the staff.

Behaviour and discipline policies must be flexible and reflect a realistic appraisal of pupils with EBD (DfEE, 1999; Richards, 1999).

Pupils who are hyperactive, and particularly those who are impulsive, can be very tiresome for peers just as much as for parents and teachers. For this reason, it is very important to try to prevent them from being rejected and socially isolated. This can be achieved partly by teaching social skills to the pupil, and partly by encouraging an atmosphere of greater tolerance in the classroom and playground (DfEE/QCA, 1999).

Academic standards, interpersonal relations and pupil self-esteem

Increasing academic attainment, developing interpersonal relations and enhancing self-esteem are triple goals of education for all pupils, and can be seen as wholly consistent with the aims of education articulated in the *Warnock Report* (DES, 1978), the Scottish *Progress Report* (SED, 1978), and the Irish *Report of the Special Education Review Committee* (Department of Education, 1993). These can be summarised as personal development – physical, intellectual, emotional, social, spiritual and moral, and the development of social relationships and entry into the world of work.

Curriculum content and organisation

Official publications on the curriculum are predicated on fundamental assumptions which include that pupils with special needs should be enabled to have access to a curriculum that meets the currently perceived needs of the majority of pupils, and the interests of the national economy (Molina y Garcia and Alban-Metcalfe, 1998). However, just as it a truism to say that we only come to understand the nature of the learning process by studying the nature of learning difficulties, it is our contention that the most valid insights into what school curricula ought to comprise will come from analysing the needs of those pupils identified as having 'special educational needs'. Such a discussion is, however, outside the scope of this book, in which shall have to satisfy ourselves with suggestions about how various kinds of curriculum organisation can enable pupils with AD/HD to succeed in an inclusive classroom.

This said, successful inclusion in primary schools has been associated, in general, with:

- detailed curriculum planning, coupled with thorough monitoring of attainment and progress;
- highest priority given to literacy, numeracy and speaking and listening;
- strong provision of art, music and drama;
- effective use of ICT;
- a clear and sustained approach to homework;
- effective use of assessment data to focus attention on individuals and groups;

at secondary level, in particular, with:

- an effective approach to literacy at Key Stage 3, which includes planning to support pupils with special educational needs (SEN);
- setting and reviewing academic targets, which are communicated to all staff and parents;
- a Key Stage 4 curriculum which meets specific needs and aspirations, e.g., through links with business and further education;
- curricular activities that extend pupils' interests, capture their imagination and enable them to develop high-level skills;
- opportunities to take responsibility and to develop personal qualities;
- provision of trained mentors to help with the organisation of work and to broaden perspectives;

and for pupils with SEN, with:

- early identification of needs and immediate intervention;
- well-qualified and well-informed SENCOs;
- effective use of ICT in diagnosis and teaching;
- effective multi-agency cooperation (OFSTED, 2000).

Successful inclusion of pupils with emotional and behavioural difficulties was promoted where there was constant striving to identify academic, non-academic and vocational qualifications best suited to pupil needs, without regard to position on league tables (Richards, 1999).

Quality of teaching

Schools that were successful in promoting inclusion were characterised by:

- teaching that was especially well planned, systematic and incremental;
- work that was purposeful and which progressed pupils' knowledge and understanding, while being within their capacity;
- activities which were motivating, enhanced their self-belief and increased their capacity to organise their work.

Effective teachers established clear and uncomplicated classroom routines, made effective use of time and resources, maintained high standards and sustained teacher-pupil interaction. Planning and assessment were carried out jointly by teachers and support staff, in relation to agreed standards, and there was a focus on in-service training (OFSTED, 2000). Success with pupils with emotional and behavioural difficulties was achieved where there was an emphasis on avoiding problems by motivating and enjoyable lessons, rather than controlling behaviour. This was supported by consistent, detailed observations, which were recorded objectively, with behaviours classified into subgroups so as to ease and strengthen analysis (DfEE, 1999; Richards, 1999).

Quality of resources

An important feature of schools that promote inclusive education is that they create a physical environment that is welcoming, is conducive to learning and reflects high expectations of attainment and behaviour. High-quality displays serve to encourage and to record learning (OFSTED, 2000). It would, however, be naïve to suggest that successful inclusion does not have resource implications, for example, in the employment of learning support staff.

Home-school and school-community links

Successful educational inclusion depends on developing strong and purposeful links between the school and the home, which are characterised by mutual respect, recognition of complementary expertise and a willingness to learn from each other (Armstrong, 1995), and between the school and the community, both local and further afield. The characteristics of effective home-school cooperation, which should be genuinely two-way (Richards, 1999), include:

- frequent and informative communication;
- ensuring that access to the school is readily available, that the atmosphere is perceived by parents as friendly and welcoming, and that the teachers are approachable and knowledgeable;
- enabling parents to participate in the life of the school, for example, by attending assemblies, or by having a meeting-place set aside for them;
- dealing immediately and in a straightforward way with urgent matters;
- a style and tone of school-home contact that is designed to unlock the parent(s) interest in what their child is doing;
- communication by the school of a consistent message about its approach to pupils' work and behaviour;
- written communication that is well presented and in which the message is expressed clearly;
- production of written reports on pupils' progress, with indications of expected standards of work;
- regular meetings with parents, which are well planned and time-tabled;
- oral and/or written guidance about ways in which parents can support their child's learning, which is explained fully;
- translation of all messages (oral and written) where appropriate;
- the effective use of home-school liaison teachers, particularly with parents who find attending meetings at school difficult or intimidating (OFSTED, 2000).

In addition, both primary and secondary schools could offer courses for parents, with a focus on:

- enabling them to be more effective in helping their own child's learning; and/or
- enabling them to provide learning support within the schools, for example, with basic skills at primary level, technical skills at secondary level.

Barriers to effective parent-teacher partnership, and ways that they can be overcome, have been discussed by Blamires, *et al.* (1997). In the case of pupils with AD/HD, there may be the need for regular, structured home-school communication on a daily or weekly basis (see Chapter 4).

School governors occupy a special position in relation to both the school and the community because, while being representatives of the local community, they are an integral part of the school (Drayton, 1999). As far as pupils with EBD are concerned, the governor with special responsibility for SEN has a vital role to play (Richards, 1999).

One of the greatest frustrations that parents of a child with AD/HD can experience is that of enabling their child to participate in out-of-school groups, such as swimming clubs (Fletcher, 1999). Although there are no simple solutions, schools should consider the extent to which they can act as a focus as well as a venue for groups that are staffed by suitably qualified – and tolerant – individuals. A computer/internet group is one possibility, though it does have the danger of encouraging isolated, rather pro-social behaviour.

Multi-agency cooperation

In view of the multifaceted nature of AD/HD, cooperation of this kind is essential and has been the subject of a recent report by the British Psychological Society (2000). The principles and practice of multi-agency working are discussed in Chapters 4 and 8.

Attitudes of staff and teacher self-esteem

The attitudes of teachers to the education of children with SEN, particularly those with AD/HD, in mainstream classrooms (Croll and Moses, 2000) and the effect of challenging behaviour on teachers' self-esteem (Lawrence, 1996), are of central importance to successful inclusion. In many cases teachers' views are based on a lack of correct information about, and/or absence of experience of working with, such children. Teacher self-esteem is profoundly affected by successful or unsuccessful classroom experience, and the way that teachers are treated by other professionals. Where inclusion of children with AD/HD is successful, it is based on a high level of teacher competence, supported by targeted INSET and positive self-esteem, and takes places in an ethos that stresses tolerance of and support for individual differences (see Chapter 8). A recent study of Greek teachers suggested that they attribute the causes of EBD more to teacher and school factors than to family and child (Poulou and Norwich, 2000). Mosley (1996) proposed a number of self-directed questions for teachers. These include: Do I genuinely like and care for each of the pupils in my class? Do I speak respectfully to them and acknowledge their positive attributes? Am I able to organise the curriculum in such a way that each pupil can gain at least some success? Am I able to apologise to a pupil if I have acted wrongly? If the answers to these questions are negative, the teacher should take steps to enhance her/his own self-esteem, to reduce stress and/or to seek professional support from colleagues.

In-service education and training; access to latest research

Good-quality targeted INSET, both that organised at a local level by schools and LEAs and that which leads to recognised qualifications, such as national qualifications for SENCOs and university degrees and diplomas, must remain a top priority in Education.

This is especially the case for AD/HD, which is only gradually coming to be recognised as a not infrequently occurring condition, the nature of which, and the implications for best practice, are the subject of ongoing research and debate. Staff at all levels should be kept up-to-date with current theory and practice.

CHAPTER 4

Helping children with AD/HD

This chapter and the following three examine in detail ways in which provision can be made for children with AD/HD, starting with identification and assessment, then considering individual educational plans and their implementation in an inclusive classroom.

Code of practice

The new *Code of Practice* for identifying and assessing pupils with SEN in England and Wales (Draft Version), comprises four stages for children of pre-school (Early Years) or school age:

Box 4.1:

Stage 1: Early Years Action/School Action

For a child who despite early education experiences or differentiated learning opportunities:

- makes little or no progress even when teaching opportunities are particularly targeted to improve the child's area of weakness;
- continues working at levels significantly below those expected of children of a similar age in certain areas;
- presents persistent emotional and/or behavioural difficulties, which are not ameliorated by the behaviour management techniques usually employed in the setting/school;
- has sensory or physical problems and continues to make little or no progress despite provision of personal aids and equipment;
- has communication and/or interaction difficulties and requires specific individual interventions in order to access learning and continues to make little or no progress despite the provision of a differentiated curriculum.

In devising strategies to enable progress, which should be recorded in an Individual Education Plan (IEP), the classteacher and special educational needs coordinator (SENCO) should seek additional information from the parents and may seek help and advice from other professionals.

Stage 2: Early Years Action Plus/School Action Plus

This stage is characterised by the involvement of external support services, who can offer advice on IEPs and targets, provide more specialist assessments, give advice on new or specialist strategies or materials and provide support for particular activities.

Stage 3: Statutory Assessment

A child can be referred to the local education authority (LEA) for a statutory assessment by the school, the parents or another agency. On receipt of a request, the LEA must decide within a period of six weeks whether or not to undertake an assessment. If the decision is Yes, the assessment must be undertaken within a further period of 10 weeks, after which the decision whether or not to write a statement must be made within a further two weeks. If a statement is to be written, a proposed statement must be written and an agreed version completed within eight weeks. Alternatively, a note in lieu must be written, setting out the reasons for not making a statement, in which case an appeal can be made to the SEN Tribunal.

The statutory assessment will be based on information about the child's learning difficulty and progress (records of reviews and their outcome; National Curriculum levels; attainment in literacy and numeracy; educational and other assessment; medical history), together with information about the special education provision made during Action Plus (IEPs; involvement of other professionals or services) and the views of the parents.

Stage 4: Statement

This must comprise: Introduction – background information; Special Educational Needs – details of each and every SEN identified during the statutory assessment and advice received; Special Educational Provision – objectives; provision; arrangements for monitoring and assessing progress; Placement – type and name of school; Non-Educational Needs, and Non-Educational Provision – involving health, social services or other agencies (DfEE, 2000a).

Corresponding arrangements are made in Scotland (Scottish Office, 1996), leading to a Record of Needs (Scottish Office, 1994), and Northern Ireland (Department of Education for Northern Ireland, 1998).

In practice, somewhere in the order of 20 per cent of pupils attending a mainstream school have been identified as having special educational needs, and are at stages 1 or 2; approximately 2 per cent of pupils with SEN have a Statement.

Identification

The symptoms of AD/HD may first be noticed by the parent or health visitor when the child is very young. The characteristics that may be observed are:

- continual restlessness;
- higher than usual level of activity;
- a very short attention span;
- motor coordination problems;
- difficulty with sleeping;
- unwillingness to be cuddled.

Commonly, though, even where symptoms have been present before age 6 years, they may only be recognised when the child goes to nursery or primary school, or in some cases only at secondary level. The need for early intervention is highlighted by the work of Sonuga-Burke and Goldfoot (1995) who found evidence of potentially negative two-way parent-child interactions, different ways of controlling the child and the risk of lowered expectations or a handling style that may exacerbate existing difficulties.

The checklist in Figure 4.1 summarises the pattern of behaviour that may occur at home and school.

Specification of how frequently a behaviour occurs is preferable to a rating scale such as, 'not at all', 'a little', 'quite a lot', 'a lot', because individual raters differ in the criteria they use (Reid and Maag, 1994). There is also evidence of cultural differences (Alban-Metcalfe, *et al.*, 2001) and inter-ethnic bias (Sonuga-Burke, *et al.*, 1993).

Assessment

Teachers and parents play a crucial role in the assessment process, which is coordinated initially by an educational or clinical psychologist and, if a diagnosis is to be made, a paediatrician or child psychiatrist.

Box 4.2

Initial identification by parent or teacher
↓
Decision to undertake an assessment (taken by school or general medical practitioner)
↓
Referral to educational or clinical psychologist, paediatrician or child psychiatrist
↓
Collection of evidence from:
Parents (parental observations; completion of checklist; background information, e.g., patterns of behaviour, sleeping habits and methods of coping; situational factors that exacerbate/reduce behaviour)
+
Teacher (teacher observations; completion of checklist; records of ability, attainment and progress and behaviour at school; situational factors that exacerbate/reduce behaviour)
+
Educational or clinical psychologist, paediatrician or child psychiatrist (observation; interview with parents; interview with child; psychological tests of intellectual functioning and visual, auditory and visual motor-processing; neurophysiological tests)
↓
Diagnosis

AD/HD – CHECKLIST – SCHOOL (or HOME)		
SYMPTOM	**FREQUENCY**	**NOTES** e.g., conditions when the behaviour occurs
Does not attend to detail when drawing or writing, or in manipulative tasks	0 1 2 3 4	
Makes careless mistakes in work or other activities at school (or in homework or when engaged in leisure activities)	0 1 2 3 4	
Finds it difficult to concentrate on work (or homework) or play activities	0 1 2 3 4	
Does not listen when being spoken to by an adult	0 1 2 3 4	
Unsuccessful in tasks that require listening to instructions	0 1 2 3 4	
Does not complete learning tasks set at school (or chores at home)	0 1 2 3 4	
Has difficulty with organising books and papers, or writing stories in sequence (or keeping toys and bedroom tidy)	0 1 2 3 4	
Avoids activities that involve thinking for her/himself	0 1 2 3 4	
Loses things that are necessary for a lesson, e.g., books, pencils (or for her/his hobby)	0 1 2 3 4	
Easily distracted by other activities in the classroom (or at home)	0 1 2 3 4	
Tends to forget which room or which group to be in (or what family or other activities have been planned)	0 1 2 3 4	
Fidgets with hands or objects on the desk (or when sitting at home or watching TV)	0 1 2 3 4	
Has great difficulty with sitting down during story time, or standing still when being talked to	0 1 2 3 4	
Tends to leave her/his seat during lessons, or place on the floor in PE or story time (or seat during mealtimes or when doing homework)	0 1 2 3 4	
Runs around excessively during class-based lessons, during PE or in the playground (or in shopping malls)	0 1 2 3 4	
Has difficulty in playing or when asked to work (or do homework) quietly	0 1 2 3 4	
Seems to be 'on the go' all or almost all the time, or may engage in physically dangerous activities	0 1 2 3 4	
Is very talkative either with the teacher or other adult, or peers in the classroom or playground	0 1 2 3 4	
Blurts out the answer to questions during instruction, explanation or question time	0 1 2 3 4	
Finds it difficult or impossible to wait her/his turn in the classroom, during PE or in the playground (or in the park)	0 1 2 3 4	
Interrupts the teacher or other adult, or peers, in the in the classroom or playground (or when parent is on the telephone)	0 1 2 3 4	
Has difficulty with written or other work in literacy, numeracy, or other subjects, even though of average intelligence	0 1 2 3 4	
Tends to work or play alone, or to have few friends in her/his class (or at home)	0 1 2 3 4	
Appears to have low self-esteem, or lacks confidence in tackling new tasks	0 1 2 3 4	
Has great difficulty in getting to sleep at night	0 1 2 3 4	
Does not like to be cuddled or tends to shun physical contact	0 1 2 3 4	
Checklist completed by: _____ Date: _____	0 = not at all; 1 = once or more per month; 2 = once or more per week; 3 = once or more per day; 4 = once or more per hour	

Figure 4.1: AD/HD Checklist

A well-documented history must be established, based on interviews with the parents and the child, from which information can be gained about the nature of the difficulties and about how the child and family have coped, and whether either have increased or decreased with time (Kewley, 1999b). The parents are the best source of knowledge about their child. Data from this source are augmented by tests of sensory, intellectual and cognitive functioning, and checklist and other information provided by the parents and the school.

The paediatrician or child psychiatrist has, (i) to determine whether the child meets enough criteria for making a diagnosis of combined or subtype AD/HD, (ii) to eliminate the possibility that the symptoms indicate a different condition (differential diagnosis), (iii) to examine the possibility that the child has both AD/HD and a co-morbid disorder. Any diagnosis of AD/HD must be based on evidence from multi-modal assessment (BPS, 2000).

Approaches to intervention

The goals of *intervention* can be summarised under three main headings:

- increasing academic attainment;
- developing interpersonal relationships, including appropriate behaviour; and
- enhancing self-esteem.

The relationships between these goals can be summarised in Figure 4.2:

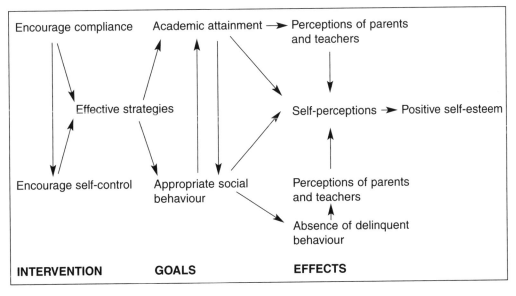

Figure 4.2: Nature and effects of intervention

As far as children with AD/HD are concerned, the question is, which of the three goals – increasing academic attainment, developing social relationships or enhancing self-esteem – should be targeted. From the teacher's point of view, it might seem most sensible to start by targeting behaviours that are disruptive to the class and annoying to the teacher, e.g., calling out in class, moving around the classroom. There are, however, reasons for not doing so (Pliszka, *et al.*, 1999). Interventions targeted at problem behaviours (e.g., off-task behaviour) were found to be successful in decreasing such behaviours, but did *not* have any effect on academic productivity. However, targeting of actual work productivity led not only to an increase in output, but also, indirectly, to a decrease in problem behaviour (Ayllon, *et al.*, 1975). Targeting attainment and behaviour in parallel is also successful (Hinshaw, *et al.*, 1998). The real dangers for these children are academic failure, and exclusion from school, with consequences that include low self-esteem, delinquency and substance abuse (Barkley, 1998).

An academic context can provide activities, which:

(a) are valued by the child, since they enable her/him to succeed in ways that are valued by the child's teacher, parents and peers, that is, her/his 'significant others';

(b) can lead to immediate rewards – initially extrinsic rewards, e.g., teacher approval, gold stars, tokens, and later rewards of an intrinsic kind, e.g., satisfaction from having succeeded at a difficult task.

The key to achieving these goals is *effective management* and *self-management strategies*, that is to say, the development of appropriate ways of dealing with people, things and events, both at home and at school, and later on at work. Such strategies can be developed in one of two ways:

1. as the result of the child responding as required to the wishes of others, in other words being compliant. This takes the form of behaving in such a way as to gain rewards and avoid punishment;

2. as the result of the child controlling her/his own actions. This takes the form of goal-directed, purposeful behaviour.

As they grow and develop, all children are encouraged to move through the stage of being compliant to that of having self-control. Achievement of academic success leads to approval by parents and teachers, just as the development of socially acceptable behaviour leads to approval by parents, peers and teachers (though sometimes on the basis of different criteria). Success in these areas leads, in turn, to enhanced self-perceptions and an enhanced self-esteem. Furthermore, increases in academic attainment often lead to better behaviour in class, and good behaviour – at least in terms of a significant amount of on-task behaviour – is, for most children, a pre-requisite for academic success.

For many children, this can be achieved without recourse to any kind of medical intervention, but for some, medication can have the effect of enabling them to be receptive to the kind of educational provision they are offered.

Behavioural and educational intervention

Behaviour management is based on the principle of 'reinforcement'. Teachers and parents give positive reinforcement – i.e., some kind of reward to the child – for behaviours that they wish to encourage, and negative reinforcement for behaviours that they wish to discourage. Negative reinforcement can take the form either of withdrawal of a positive reinforcer, e.g., not smiling at the child, not paying attention to what s/he is doing, or of administering some kind of punishment, which can range from a mild rebuke to 'time-out', when the child is prevented for doing a chosen activity (Robin, 1998; Teeter, 1998).

Educational interventions commonly use behaviour management techniques, but what sets them apart in this instance are (a) an emphasis on changing the circumstances presented to the child in order to prevent the undesired behaviour, coupled with (b) interacting with the child in such a way as to ensure that the child is engaged in meaningful activities. At home, such activities include recreation and leisure; at school, they include structured play among younger children and involvement in learning activities that the child or adolescent finds intrinsically interesting, supported by active encouragement and enabling her/him to remain on-task.

The principles governing successful educational intervention include:

- clarity and precision when presenting learning tasks;
- careful structuring and sequencing of learning tasks;
- involving the pupil in designing and monitoring learning tasks;
- frequent feedback on performance, along with prompts to remain on-task;
- taking care about the placement of the pupil in relation to other individuals in the classroom;
- minimising external distracters;
- establishing organisational structures, and simple and easy-to-follow rules and routines;
- ensuring that any request made involves the child in being active, rather than inactive (Cooper and Ideus, 1996; DuPaul and Stoner, 1994).

In many cases, behavioural and educational intervention alone is enough to achieve success.

Medical intervention

Some children do not respond to behavioural and educational intervention alone, and significant changes in their behaviour can only be brought about using this in combination with drugs (Hinshaw, *et al.*, 1998; Kewley, 1999a, b). The drugs currently licensed for the treatment of AD/HD, only for children aged 6 years and above, are methylphenidate ('Ritalin') and dexamphetamine ('Dexedrine'), though tricyclic and other antidepressants are sometimes prescribed. Following expert diagnosis, drug prescription and patient monitoring may be undertaken by a GP, but only under shared care arrangements with the specialist (NICE, 2000). The principles underlying the use of drugs are:

- they affect children's neurophysiological processing by stimulating those centres that have a controlling effect on behaviour;
- they provide a window of opportunity to enable the child to be receptive to appropriate behavioural and educational provision.

The arguments for and against the use of drugs are discussed in Chapter 8, though it should be noted here that drugs should be complementary to, rather than a substitute for, non-medical intervention.

Individual Education Plans

An Individual Education Plan (IEP) should include the following information: (DfEE, 2000a; see also Scottish Office, 1994)

- the short-term targets set for the child;
- the teaching strategies to be used;
- the provision to be put in place;
- when the plan is to be reviewed;
- the outcome of the actions taken.

A useful way of presenting the information for an IEP is to use a *Proforma* of the kind shown in Figure 4.3, in which interventions are grouped in terms of academic attainment, interpersonal relations including behaviour in class, and self-esteem.

At secondary school, it is necessary to modify the IEP for the different subjects taught. Examples of IEPs are given in Chapters 5, 6 and 7.

Figure 4.3: Proforma for Individual Education Plan (extracts for actual IEPs are given in chapters 5, 6 and 7).

Name of pupil: DOB:	IEP completed by: Date:

Learning/behavioural characteristics	

Detailed description of the child's learning/behavioural difficulties, based on:

- Formal and informal observations by teacher, Learning Support Assistant (LSA), etc.;
- Evidence from other professionals, e.g., educational or clinical psychologist, paediatrician or child psychiatrist;
- Observations by parents;
- Child's own perceptions, including self-monitoring data,

plus general background information about the child.

This will specify information about inattentive, hyperactive and/or impulsive behaviour, and information about academic attainment and progress, social relations (including behaviour in class), self-esteem.

Other information, e.g., *child's cognitive style and preferred learning style, interests, motivation, approach to learning, potential peer support, family background.*

Intervention: (a) targets		
Academic	**Interpersonal and behavioural**	**Self-esteem**
(a) **long term**	(a) **long term**	(a) **long term**
(b) **short term**	(b) **short term**	(b) **short term**
Academic targets to be met in terms of level of attainment and rate of progress.	Targets in relation to (a) interpersonal relations with peers and others, (b) general behaviour in class.	Focus areas for enhancing self-esteem.
Criteria for success and time scale.	Criteria for success and time scale.	Criteria for success and time scale.

Intervention: (b) strategies		
Academic	**Interpersonal and behavioural**	**Self-esteem**
Action to be taken in terms of: <ul><li>kind of special provision to be made;</li><li>staff to be involved, e.g., LSA, including the frequency of their intervention;</li><li>any specific academic programmes, activities, materials or equipment to be used.</li></ul>	Action to be taken in terms of: <ul><li>kind of special provision to be made;</li><li>staff to be involved, e.g., LSA, including the frequency of their intervention;</li><li>any specific social/behavioural programmes, activities, materials or equipment to be used.</li></ul>	Action to be taken in terms of: <ul><li>kind of special provision to be made;</li><li>staff to be involved, e.g., LSA, including the frequency of their intervention;</li><li>any specific academic or social activities, materials or equipment to be used.</li></ul>

Relevant documentation and other educational, pastoral or medical requirements
Reports from class teacher and other professionals, including: assessment data; reports of review meetings; reports to parents. Information about additional provision to be made, *e.g., for speech and language therapy, psychotherapy, medication (including size and frequency of dosage).*

Staff involved	
Class teacher: LSA:	SENCO: Other professionals:

Monitoring and assessment
Arrangements for monitoring and assessing attainment and progress: • within the school; • with other professionals; • with parents. Report of attainment and progress.

Home-school links
Information – to be completed in close cooperation with the parents – about: • support from home, e.g., any particular help available with homework; • nature and timing of communication between home and school, e.g., amount of detail, agreed frequency (daily, weekly, monthly) – see also Proforma in Figure 4.4.

School-home links

The success of any policy of inclusive education depends on the quantity and quality of communication between the school and the home, which for some children should take place on a daily basis, though for others it can be time-tabled for once a week. The stages for establishing and maintaining the link are described below.

Stage A: A meeting should be set up between – at the very least – the parents, the class teacher, the Special Educational Needs Co-ordinator (SENCO) and the Learning Support Assistant (LSA), if there is one. It would be very valuable for other relevant professionals to be present, for example, there may be need for input from a social worker. If old enough, the child should be present at the meeting. Such meetings enable high-quality inter-agency or multi-professional support (BPS, 2000; DfEE, 2000a; Holowenko, 1999).

The meeting should share information about the nature of the diagnosis and any recommendations made by any of the parties present. For example, the educational or clinical psychologist can explain the nature of AD/HD, the effect of any medical and/or behavioural/educational treatment that is proposed and the principles upon which intervention is based; the parents can provide information about the child's behaviour at home and any home context factors that may affect successful intervention; the social worker or family therapist can explain ways in which social services may be able to offer support to the family; the headteacher or SENCO can explain how the school's policies are implemented at a whole-school level; the class teacher and LSA can explain how the school's policies are implemented through classroom practice. If a Statement has been written, the way in which its requirements can be fulfilled should also be considered and appropriate action agreed.

The kind of contextual information that the parents can provide may include: any routines that have been established, e.g., whether either parent is present when the child comes home from school; whether mealtimes precede or follow recreation time; what kind of recreation the child enjoys; what kind of support the parents can offer in relation to homework, enabling or encouraging recreation activities, enabling or encouraging social interaction with friends, or in joining clubs; child's sleeping pattern; how the parents currently manage their child's behaviour. Such information can form the basis of an agreed school-home plan, which may involve changes in, for example, certain routines and certain aspects of behaviour management at home.

Stage B: The class teacher and SENCO should discuss, in detail, the content of the IEP. A meeting of this kind can lead to the articulation of learning outcomes, and ways in which the school and the parents jointly can help the child to achieve them.

This meeting should result in:

- *identification* of those learning outcomes which the parents can help their child to achieve. Some of these will be academic, some will be behavioural. Initially, the focus will be on enabling the child to achieve, coupled with controlling the child, gradually the emphasis will be on encouraging and enabling the development of self-control;
- *specification* of ways in which the teacher and the parents can work in cooperation so that each reinforces the actions of the other. The proposed targets for the child to achieve, and the actions to be carried out by the parents, should be written down and the extent to which targets have been achieved should be evaluated after a period of four to six weeks;
- *specification* of the criteria by which success is to be judged. The number of targets should be limited in number – certainly to a maximum of three or four;

SCHOOL-HOME PROFORMA		
Child: Teacher:		Date:
Academic		Comment by teacher
e.g., during Literacy Hour – *Had all necessary equipment* *Spent most of the lesson on-task* *Completed all/most of work set*	Y ? N n/a Y ? N n/a Y ? N n/a	
Social relations		
e.g., during Literacy Hour – *Spoke during Circle Time* *Took part in role-play activity* *Shared equipment with others*	Y ? N n/a Y ? N n/a Y ? N n/a	
Behaviour		
e.g., during Literacy Hour – *Put up hand before speaking* *Remained seated during plenary* *Obeyed teacher requests*	Y ? N n/a Y ? N n/a Y ? N n/a	
Homework set:		
Time allocated:		
Time actually taken:		
Comment by parent (s) Signature		

Figure 4.4: School-home Proforma

- *agreement* about the way in which school-home and home-school communication should take place. This can be achieved using a 'School-Home Proforma' of the kind described in Figure 4.4, which should comprise information about tasks that the child should carry out at home;
- *agreement* about the kind of reinforcement that should be used at school and at home. The class teacher should describe the range of methods that s/he proposes to use – with the emphasis on much positive reinforcement – and try to ensure that comparable methods be used at home. An important aspect of school-home communication can be that the parents are able to give the child positive reinforcement of what s/he has achieved at school, and *vice versa*. However, reinforcement of this kind is likely to be less effective than reinforcement given immediately following the behaviour itself, owing to the delay, and there will therefore be a much weaker link between action and reinforcement (DuPaul and Stoner, 1994). Parents should be encouraged to use the same kind of reinforcers as those used at school and to refrain, as far as possible, from over-reliance on material rewards, which can lose their potency over time.

Stage C: Dates should be set for meetings to take place on a regular basis, certainly once a term, perhaps half-termly, to monitor progress and to propose future goals and targets.

School-Home Communication

There is a certain number of principles that should guide school-home communication. These include that:

- the nature and purpose of the home-school link should be agreed by the parents;
- the child's input about goals and targets, and about contingencies, should be sought, particularly among older children and adolescents;
- goals and targets should be communicated in a positive way;
- the goals/targets should include academic attainment, social relations and behaviour;
- only a small number of goals should be targeted at a time;
- information from the teacher should be qualitative as well as quantitative;
- the context (e.g., during Literacy Hour, or during the morning session after play) should be stated;
- communication should be regular (daily or weekly);
- home-based contingencies should be linked to attainment and behaviour at school;
- goals and contingencies should be modified, as appropriate (cf. Cooper and Ideus, 1996; DuPaul and Stoner, 1994).

CHAPTER 5

Increasing academic attainment

Case study 1: Adrian – IEP (extract) (first part)
Age 8 years – diagnosed at age 5 years as having AD/HD Combined-type, prescribed Ritalin – speech and language: delay in expressive, but not receptive language; when tested at age 5 was below the 5th percentile on British Ability Scales (BAS) for matrices and similarities; behaviour: verbally abusive, fights a lot (at school and home).

Current areas of concern: very short attention span; makes careless mistakes; great difficulty with organising his work; difficulty with remaining in his seat; interrupts teacher and other pupils frequently; learning difficulties in literacy (Speaking and listening L2, Reading L1, Writing L1) and mathematics (L1 in each area, except Space and shape L2); auditory and sequential memory delay; behaviour: verbally abusive, fights a lot (at school and home).

Strengths: practical work in Design Technology, and Art and Design; has a good memory for facts in History; able to predict what will happen in drama activities; quick at learning and able to remember telephone numbers (information from parents).

The information given is valuable in that it records, (i) performance data from age 5 and currently; (ii) inattentive, hyperactive and impulsive behaviours of particular concern; (iii) areas of strength in school work; and (iv) general behaviour, and is based on observations from both home and school. There is, however, (i) no indication of the dosage of Ritalin, when it is to be taken, and whether either has been modified, nor (ii) the nature of any parental support.

The evidence presented in Chapter 2 suggests seven conclusions that can be drawn about children with AD/HD. These are:

1. that they experience difficulties which are a direct consequence of the way in which they process information – some aspects of their processing of information do not function efficiently. For example, a deficit in working memory makes it difficult for a child to do addition or take-away sums, when lots of numbers are involved;

2. that some of these information-processing difficulties are more far reaching in their effect. For example, deficits in using foresight and hindsight, particularly when coupled with a working memory deficit, make it difficult for a child to organise and plan academic tasks. Deficits of this kind also cause difficulty in social situations, owing to an inability to predict accurately how others will act;

3. that – by way of contrast – some children with AD/HD do show very high levels of competence on tasks that require a high level of skill, such as model making, caring for a pet animal and information-processing skills, such as those involved in using a computer;

4. that they experience difficulty in controlling their behaviour, which shows itself both in difficulty with remaining on-task, and in achieving rule governed behaviour;

5. that some of their difficulty in controlling own behaviour manifests itself in lack of motivation to do certain tasks, notably those tasks which hold no intrinsic interest to the child;

6. that – again by way of contrast – when engaged in activities of their own choosing, children with AD/HD are commonly reported to be highly motivated to remain on-task, even to the point of excessive perseveration;

7. that they are likely to have very low self-esteem.

The principal areas of difficulties are, therefore, in the areas of: academic attainment, interpersonal relations, self-esteem.

Some of the difficulties that children with AD/HD experience with academic tasks and in social situations are a direct consequence of deficits in their information-processing capacities, while others are motivational in original. In other words, while sometimes they do not achieve because they are unable, sometimes they do not achieve because they do not wish to try – sometimes it's 'can't do', sometimes it's 'could do, but don't want to'. Either way, their self-esteem suffers.

In planning intervention, it is necessary to be clear about: (a) the academic goals that are to be achieved, in the short, medium and long term; (b) the range of teaching strategies and techniques that are available and their effectiveness; (c) the kinds of teaching-learning activities and resources that promote effective learning; (d) the ways in which modifications to the learning environment can make teaching more effective; and (e) the criteria against which attainment and progress can be measured. For teaching and learning to be effective – particularly among children with AD/HD – parents and teachers must share the same goals.

Principles and practice

For children with AD/HD, many of the principles and much good practice are the same as for all other children. Some principles and practice, however, apply uniquely to children who are inattentive, impulsive and/or hyperactive, but can nevertheless be applied in an inclusive classroom (e.g., Cooper and Ideus, 1996; Cooper, 1999; DuPaul and Stoner, 1994; Webster-Stratton, 1999).

General principles and practice

Positive engagement Children's refusal to engage on a task is often owing to previous unsuccessful attempts at similar tasks, with consequent failure and humiliation. Tasks should, therefore, be interesting and achievable.

Positive atmosphere An atmosphere in which the teacher adopts a 'solution focus', rather than a focus on identifying the source of problems and apportioning blame, serves as a model of pupil behaviour.

Positive interactions Teacher-child behaviour should be characterised by warmth and friendliness, showing empathy and unconditional positive regard. Humour, but never irony, can be used to good effect, particularly as it signals a teacher's respect for a child, who is being treated as an intellectual equal. This can have a beneficial effect on self-esteem.

Positive attention For all children, any attention – even being told off – is better than no attention. Success in minimising undesirable and negative behaviour lies in maximising desirable and positive behaviour by noticing and rewarding it, by catching children being good.

Communication Clarity of communication and willingness to listen are essential. Clear and effective communication may require information and instructions to be repeated and paraphrased. Children should be asked to repeat what was said in their own words. Children will feel empowered if encouraged to ask questions if unclear about information/instructions and if encouraged to explain the reasons for their actions when they are accused of doing something wrong. It may, of course, transpire that they were right!

Individual differences It is also essential that teachers be aware of individual learner characteristics, both in relation to their strengths, as well as areas for development, and to their

preferred modes and styles of learning. Children with AD/HD show a marked preference for active, 'hands-on' or practical learning activities.

Differentiation This can be in a number of ways. These include: by content – a reading programme might stress auditory processing for some children, language enrichment for
others; pace – where children carry out the same activities, but at different rates; level –
small-group activities in numeracy would be set at different levels of difficulty; mode of
delivery – teacher's use of different channels (visual, auditory, kinaesthetic) to present
information; mode of response – children's use of different methods (oral, written,
diagrammatic) to present information; cognitive and learning style – preference for kind
of processing (e.g., auditory, visual, kinaesthetic; sequential, simultaneous; top-down and
bottom-up learning); teaching style – demonstration, question and answer, discussion,
etc.; grouping – whole class, small group, pairs (DfEE, 2000b; Lewis, 1992).

Self-esteem This can be protected and nurtured if tasks are designed such that there are
opportunities for success, leading to a sense of competence and recognition of what has
been achieved, leading to confidence (see Chapter 7).

Specific principles and practice

Recognising the importance of language Children with AD/HD have difficulties in auditory
processing and using private speech. Thus, teachers need to ensure that instructions and
information given orally are brief and uncomplicated. It is useful to summarise information in written or picture form. Teachers can encourage the development of private
speech, which children use as one of the strategies for controlling their actions in academic and social contexts, by modelling and scaffolding its effective use. (An example of
scaffolding in practice is given on p. 74). As noted in Chapter 2, ability to use private language affects rule-governed behaviour.

Rules Owing to difficulties with language, rules should be expressed graphically as well as
in written form, with visual and/or experiential examples that are relevant to the child.
Teachers should not assume that all children possess the linguistic skills necessary to
understand verbal rules, or to express their feelings about them.

Routines It is important for children with AD/HD that their lives have regular patterns,
and the behaviour of others be predictable. This enables them to internalise such patterns
as a first stage to being able to reduce their deficit in foresight and thus anticipate the
effects of their actions, and so gain a measure of predictive control over their environment. It is important that routines be uncomplicated and that the child understand how
they fit into the overall structure of the day.

Level of stimulation There is the danger that children with AD/HD may be overstimulated, particularly when working in a large group. For this reason, they should be given opportunities to work in pairs, rather than in a group situations. Care should be taken in then choice of partner. When working in a group is judged appropriate, care should be taken to structure the experience such that the child with AD/HD is placed with a group that is skilled in cooperation and collaboration, if possible, on an activity to which s/he can make a valuable contribution. In general, such children work best where there is quiet and calm and may even need to have a designated place to work, for example, with a screen.

Susceptibility to distraction There is the need to place the child at a desk from which materials irrelevant to the task have been removed, and in a location that is free from distractions but where the teacher can observe off-task behaviour. Having said this, provision of an environment that is totally stimulus-free would be counterproductive, because, under conditions of 'sensory deprivation', a child with AD/HD will become distracted with her/his own thoughts. The key to success, is sharply delineated and highly focused tasks.

Learning tasks Tasks should be broken down into a number of small subtasks, each of which has a clear and meaningful focus, and – so as to maintain interest – the content of each should be stimulating and the types of subtask varied. The expectations and criteria for success should be shared with the pupil. Following success, the length and complexity of tasks can be increased.

Active learning Children with AD/HD enjoy and gain most benefit from tasks in which they are *active* participants. For this reason, activities in which they have to take a passive role should be limited in number and duration. During story time, or other receptive learning activities, a hyperactive child is likely to benefit from being allowed to carry out an activity, such as drawing or doodling, at the back of the class. The 'dead-man test for behaviour' (Lindsley, 1991) is relevant here: if a dead person could do it, it wasn't behaviour. Thus, commands such as, 'Sit still', should be replaced by, 'Sit still and try to guess what will happen next'.

Monitoring progress When monitoring the progress that a pupil is making, it is important to concentrate attention on the task itself rather than on the pupil's behaviour. Thus, the focus should be on performance and products, for example, what the pupil is doing to achieve the goal, or the amount of work completed, rather than on whether or not s/he remains in her/his seat. Close monitoring of what the pupil is achieving, and the methods used, is essential in the identification of learning difficulties and planning appropriate action.

Difficulties in learning Owing to difficulties with processing information, for example in sequencing, children with AD/HD may have specific difficulties with writing and other tasks, which are additional to problems with concentrating over a period of time. Thus, they need specific and sustained help on tasks that involve short-term or working memory and organisation. They also benefit both from previews of what they are about to do – explanation of the task and of likely rewards – and from reviewing their achievements. These help in the development of foresight and hindsight.

Frequency of reinforcement The predominant form of reinforcement should be positive (praise, or other rewards), which should significantly outweigh the negative (ignoring, or other punishments). However, unlike other children, those with AD/HD have difficulty in maintaining their behaviour when reinforcement is intermittent. This means that, in addition to being specific and targeted, the feedback they receive should be relatively continuous. Rewards should also be small and immediate, rather than large and delayed. This serves to prompt their working memory, to keep them on-task, to satisfy their need for reassurance, and to bolster their self-esteem.

Types of reinforcement Positive reinforcers are only effective if they are desired by the pupil. This means that what the pupil wants should first be determined, either through observation or conversation. However, in view of the phenomenon or 'reinforcement fatigue' among children with AD/HD, a range or 'menu' of rewards should be available.

Teaching and learning activities

While recognising, (i) that child development is a continuous process, and (ii) that children differ both in their individual learner characteristics and needs and in their rate of development, it is nevertheless convenient to divide the educational process into phases. As Table 5.1 indicates, most teaching-learning activities have their foundations in an earlier stage and continue into the next stage.

For children with AD/HD, there is often the need to encourage and to enable them to participate effectively in activities that many other children engage in spontaneously. In many cases, this can be achieved through teaching-learning activities that are relevant to all pupils in the class; in other cases, specific activities need to be developed.

Table 5.1 Teaching-learning activities

PRE-SCHOOL AND EARLY YEARS	JUNIOR YEARS	SECONDARY YEARS
Play **Pre-academic and basic skills** **Speech and language** **Sequencing and organisational skills** **Beginning of metacognitive awareness** **Problem solving** **Creative subjects**	**Play** **Basic skills** **Speech and language** **Organisational and study skills** **Metacognition** **Problem solving** **Creative subjects**	**Play** **Basic skills** **Speech and language** **Organisational and study skills** **Metacognition** **Problem solving** **Creative subjects** **Career planning and vocational skills**
The development of pre-academic and basic skills depends, among other things, upon the child's ability: • to concentrate on what is said; • to remember it over a period of time; • to think about what was said; and • to organise and plan to express ideas in a way that can be understood (Reif, 1993; Teeter, 1998).	The transition into later junior and secondary education places increasing demands on: • obtaining information from printed materials; • obtaining information from formal lessons; • demonstrating knowledge and understanding through tests; • expressing information in writing; • working independently; • using a broad range of cognitive and metacognitive strategies; • interacting appropriately with same and opposite sex peers and adults; and • having a motivation to learn (Mercer and Mercer, 1993; Robin, 1998).	

1. Play

The educational significance of play cannot be overestimated. At a cognitive level, play stimulates language and speech, leads to increased knowledge and understanding of the world, encourages the use of imagination and reasoning, involves problem-solving activities and leads to cognitive development in general. In addition, it provides a context for the expression of feelings and emotions, for resolving inner conflicts and anxieties, for developing self-confidence and self-control, and is itself intrinsically motivating (Bennett, *et al.*, 1997). It is important not to think of play as the exclusive domain of children since quite the opposite is true. Among adults just as much as children, the ability to play is an integral part of development, both recreational and work-related. Playing with ideas, as in brainstorming during problem solving and creativity, is essential if the best solutions are to be found. When she agreed to take over a Year 6 class, one teacher, who for the previous five years had taught in Reception class, demanded that there should be a sand tray and a water trough in her new classroom. What she firmly believed – as was borne out in practice – was that 10- and 11-year-old children benefit from trying their ideas out in practice, rather than being forced into the 'abstract world' that constitutes much of the Key Stage 2 (and Key Stages 3 and 4) curriculum. This is especially true for children with AD/HD, for whom active learning is most effective. However, play – which is both a process and a product – is an area of generic competence that such children need to be taught, in both pre-academic and social contexts.

Play, which is not exclusive to the sand tray, the water trough, the role play area and the playground, also takes place during 'Quality Circle Time' (Mosley, 1996), and as 'playing with ideas' as part of many lessons, among children of all ages.

Unfortunately, in most early years classrooms play is relegated to second place to the more 'serious' business of developing the basic skills of literacy and numeracy. The reasons for this are, in part: (i) teachers' lack of knowledge and understanding of how to enable effective learning to take place through this medium; (ii) that, for learning through play to be effective, it is costly in adult time; and (iii) pressure from central government.

General strategies

A valuable distinction has been drawn between 'ludic' (or fun-orientated) and 'epistemic' (or learning-orientated) play (Hutt, *et al.*, 1989). While all children benefit from teacher intervention in developing their epistemic play, through guided-discovery and 'scaffolded' learning (Bennett, *et al.*, 1997; Monighan-Nouret, *et al.*, 1987), children with AD/HD need help with ludic play as well.

Active engagement Among most children, play is characterised by an unwillingness to be distracted from a chosen activity. Therefore, part of the teacher's role is to provide a range of activities that will enable the child to learn about the world through the Piagetian process of structured guided-discovery learning. However, many children engage in desultory activities of little of no value. Even where the emphasis is on learning by discovery, there is the need for much high-quality adult-child interaction, which includes complex play activities and lively and purposeful learning (Meadows and Cashdan, 1988). There is, therefore, also a need for active intervention by the teacher, both to stimulate the child to think in different ways, and to develop new knowledge and skills. Here, Vygotsky's (1978) concept of 'scaffolding', whereby the teacher, (i) models the activity to be learnt, (ii) encourages the child to perform the activity at the same time, with teacher help, (iii) gradually reduces the amount of help given ('fading'), and (iv) encourages the child to work independently is particularly valuable for children with AD/HD.

Intrinsic motivation This can be thought of as a genuine desire to act in a certain way. For most children, the objects provided by the teacher include some that engage their attention over quite long periods of time. The teacher's role is to provide an appropriate range. In the case of children with AD/HD, it is important to ensure that the materials themselves are stimulating in a visual, auditory or tactile way.

Means and ends Children are less concerned with particular goals than with the various means of reaching them. For example, once a child has solved a jigsaw puzzle, s/he may use the pieces to build a house, and then use one of them as a pretend aeroplane. Such shifting among different patterns of means and goals is thought to contribute to flexibility in thinking and problem solving. In contrast, because children with AD/HD tend to move from one activity to another, without developing or extending any of them, they need more encouragement to think, for example, of how the same object can be used in different ways, and in their case imaginative play should be modelled.

Non-literal behaviour Pre-school play shows children's capacity to transform objects and situations to conform to their play themes, as in the pretend aeroplane above. This capacity to 'make-believe' is thought to contribute to the use of abstract symbols, as in reading and number work, to understanding symbolic behaviour during role play, and to engagement in hypothetical or 'as-if' thinking, required in problem-solving – all areas in which children with AD/HD have difficulties. Here they, more than other children, need specific, targeted teacher input within the context of play.

Speech and language The development of speech and language is discussed on p. 54.

Specific strategies

In addition to what is provided for all children, children with AD/HD need specific input in certain areas, particularly in relation to sustained attention and organisation.

Attention span Play provides an opportunity for extending the span of focused attention, which is one of the principal goals for children with AD/HD. This can be done initially in relation to play activities chosen by the child, either by the teacher being directly involved in the task, for example, by asking questions designed to stimulate the child to think in different ways, or by maintaining an active supervisory interest. In this way, s/he can learn to anticipate and control the child's level of cognitive arousal and enable and encourage patterns of on-task behaviour. The same strategies can gradually be applied to more work-like tasks.

Knowledge and pre-academic skills Partly because of their inattentiveness and partly because of difficulty with processing information, children with AD/HD often have the added problem of deficits in their knowledge and skills base, which puts them at an additional disadvantage at school. For this reason, teachers need to be extra vigilant when carrying out baseline and other assessments on entry to school, and to target extra help in this area.

Metacognitive awareness Most children of pre-school age and younger become aware of what they know and can do – their capacities and limitations – and also of the effect of their actions on others. This awareness shows itself in knowing when to ask for help and in ability to engage in role-play activities, which involves the capacity to formulate and abide by rules. Help for children with AD/HD comes from teaching self-monitoring and role play.

Self-monitoring This can begin with the teacher asking the child about their thoughts and feelings, and about things that the child can or cannot do, does or does not understand. This is the beginning of developing a 'metacognitive perspective', which can be followed by asking the child about what other children can do, and how they feel. This promotes the development of hindsight.

Role play The development of role-play activities is characterised by an ability to negotiate roles and to develop rules based on shared verbal and non-verbal communication. The teacher can help children with AD/HD by explaining the meaning of actions and by structuring simple role-play situations, thus encouraging the development of foresight (see Chapter 6).

2. Pre-academic skills and basic skills

Almost all children of nursery and reception class age have difficulty with tasks of this kind, but it is important to identify those children who are experiencing greater difficulty than others. Teachers do, therefore, have to be vigilant, particularly during the transition from relatively simple pre-academic skills to the more complex skills required in literacy and numeracy. Such skills require ability to concentrate, to remember, to think, to organise and plan, and to express ideas; but as children progress, they have to deal with tasks that are more complex and of extended duration.

In some cases, children with AD/HD are unable to carry out certain tasks because they have not developed the necessary knowledge and understanding, skills and strategies. They have a low level of competence in one or more areas. In other cases, they are capable of doing a task, but are not motivated to do so. Indeed, many such children do show high levels of competence when they are engaged in one of their hobbies or interests, but do not engage in work at school. Or, when they do engage in school work, it is because they are receiving a social reward, such as much teacher attention, or some other kind of reinforcement (BPS, 1996).

Once again, many teaching-learning strategies that are valuable for children with AD/HD are appropriate for the whole class, others are specific to them (Barkley, 1998; Cooper, 1999; Cooper and Ideus, 1996; DuPaul and Stoner, 1994; Goldstein and Goldstein, 1990; Robin, 1998; Teeter, 1998; Webster-Stratton, 1999).

General strategies

Gaining and focusing attention Give clear commands, such as 'Freeze' and/or clear signals to gain attention, e.g., ringing a bell. Use mystery box, or an interesting story, when introducing new topics; encourage pupils to make predictions. Provide multi-sensory input when giving instructions or explanations, e.g., visual-plus-verbal, verbal-plus-gesture. Give demonstrations and active presentations. Make use of audio-visual equipment.

Maintaining attention and reducing distractions Arrange classroom so that it includes quiet areas, for example, by setting up carrels.

Language Repeat instructions and explanations in different ways, using different intonations and emphases. Encourage pupils to work in pairs or small groups. Use diagrams when giving instructions and explanations.

Processing skills Give pupils opportunities for structured and unstructured play. Identify main themes and emphasise important learning points. Encourage pupils to summarise or paraphrase teacher instructions and explanations. Repeat instructions, using different phraseology. Give verbal explanations of visual material, and use visual material to enhance oral instructions and explanations. Prioritise tasks and activities.

Concept formation Teach pupils to use concept maps (initial concept, main features, other features, positive and negative examples, links, etc.). Encourage pupils to explain their ideas or to give examples, and ask 'How?' and 'Why?' questions.

Short-term or working memory Repeat instructions. Devise clear and explicit worksheets with a combination of text and diagrams. Display class rules, both verbally and graphically.

Long-term memory Ask open-ended questions, to which there can be more than one correct answer, followed by more specific 'probing' questions.

Specific strategies

Gaining and focusing attention Make eye contact with the child when giving commands. Colour code keywords and phrases. Emphasise each of the stages in problem-solving tasks. Use subtle signalling techniques, e.g., tap on shoulder, to keep pupil on-task. Give pupil advanced warning when a new activity is about to start. Recognise that a pupil may be overwhelmed by a lot of information presented at the same time.

Maintaining attention and reducing distractions Set pupil small amounts of work, with short breaks. Devise activities which involve multi-sensory input, e.g., visual-plus-tactile, verbal-plus-tactile. Ensure removal of irrelevant material. Allow the child the use of a 'wriggle' zone, i.e., somewhere to move around if the tension gets too great. During story time, encourage pupil to keep hands busy, e.g., drawing, doodling.

Language Do not cause embarrassment if pupil misunderstands a question or request. Make a permanent record (in written and/or diagram form) of what the pupil has to do. Teach pupil to develop visual representations of verbal instructions. Practise phonic awareness using music and rhyme activities. Encourage the child to describe what s/he sees.

Processing skills Teach the child how to play in structured and unstructured situations. Give brief and concise instructions, and help her/him to stay on tasks by verbal encouragement or redirection. Break tasks down into smaller units, emphasising key learning points. Use reminder cards and tape-record some sessions. Enhance visual processing through artwork and ask the child to describe diagrams and pictures. Encourage the use of her/his strongest modality (verbal, visual, tactile) and preferred mode of learning (sequential, simultaneous). Help top-down learners to identify key factors, by underlining or listing critical events. Help bottom-up learners to be more divergent and creative in their thinking. Encourage self-monitoring, using self-report checklists.

Concept formation Check that the child understands all instructions and explanations. Ask her/him to explain tasks set, before s/he begins and during the task, and to say afterwards what s/he has learnt. Encourage use of concept maps for all new tasks.

Short-term or working memory Sit the child close to you or the LSA, so that s/he can ask questions. Ask her/him to repeat all instructions in her/his own words. Allow more time on tasks and reduce number of items in tasks. Provide, or encourage the child to prepare and use, prompt cards or cues during problem-solving activities. Allow use of calculators or word processors.

Long-term memory Give the child advanced warning before asking a question; allows more time to respond. Be selective in what needs to be remembered.

3. Speech and language

Speech and language not only provide the means by which we communicate with others, but they are also – in the form of language as a vehicle for our thoughts, and self-directed or private speech – the principal means by which we, (a) process information, and (b) regulate our own behaviour. Teachers' observations of children can provide a valuable source of information about, (i) children's receptive and expressive language, and (ii) the extent to which they use private speech.

Speech and language is an area in which children with AD/HD commonly have difficulty. Indeed, there is evidence to suggest that almost one-third of children who have a significant speech-language delay develop problems with inattention and hyperactivity (Cantwell and Baker, 1991). Furthermore, subtle as well as complex language problems may go unidentified among pre-school children, with the delays attributed to problems of behaviour or self-control. The consequence of this may be that unrealistic demands are placed on the child, who may respond with temper tantrums and even a chronic pattern of problems with behaviour, inattention and arousal-level (Goldstein and Goldstein, 1990).

General strategies

Receptive and expressive language It is essential, particularly among younger children, that they understand the nature and requirements of all tasks that are set, and that teachers listen carefully to what children say. This can be a valuable source of diagnostic information.

Private speech Although great emphasis is placed on children's acquisition of skills – for example, their ability to understand what is said to them and to express their ideas coherently – insufficient attention seems to be paid to the acquisition of strategies, such as the use of private speech in organising and planning tasks.

Specific strategies

Receptive and expressive language As with dyslexia, the oral instructions that a child can follow, and the way they express their ideas, can provide valuable information about their cognitive processing. A speech and language therapist's action plan for children identified as having difficulties can be delivered within the context of play or basic skills learning.

Private speech Most children commonly use, initially, 'outer speech' and later 'inner speech', as a strategy for regulating their behaviour (Vygotsky, 1978). Children with AD/HD need to be taught to develop this strategy. Here, the teacher's use of 'scaffolding' good practice is extremely important, particularly in tasks, such as sequencing activities, which involve imposing a structure, i.e., organisation and planning.

4. Organisational and study skills

Owing to deficits in working memory and their reduced capacity to use hindsight and foresight, children with AD/HD tend to experience great difficulty with: (a) tasks that involve the processing of a lot of information, and/or are extended in time; (b) using previous experience to deal with current tasks; and (c) predicting the outcome of stories or other series of events. The processing involves attention to auditory, visual or tactile input, working memory and cognitive and metacognitive processing, plus control of fine motor movements, written expression and spelling.

General strategies

Organisation and planning Teach children strategies for learning, for example, to preview and to plan tasks. Encourage them to use estimation skills. Ask 'What if ... ?' questions. Teach them how to organise their work, and how to use strategies for tackling new tasks. Review and evaluate alternative strategies before starting a new task.

Time management skills Encourage pupils to estimate how long tasks will take and then check time taken. Teach the effective use of calendars and planners. Encourage use of 'To-Do' lists.

Specific strategies

Organisation and planning Give the child specific help on how to use strategies for learning. Give specific help on how to devise and use strategies, and help in thinking through, in detail, the consequences of actions. Teach the pupil to analyse actions, in terms of what caused them, how they affected people and events and what could have been done differently. Teach self-assessment: What is the task? What am I trying to achieve? How am I doing? Use colour-coded workbooks. Establish good home-school liaison over class-work and homework.

Homework Ensure that the child knows the purpose of the homework, and the criteria for success. For older children agree a weekly homework plan. Set short, well-focused assignments. Encourage the pupil to write homework assignments in a special book, to be shown to parent(s). Accept assignments that are handed-in late. Assess the content rather than the presentation of work. Encourage peer tutoring that includes reminding about work to complete. Consider allowing the child to keep a second copy of textbooks at home.

Note taking Allocate a low-distraction work area and stand near the child during the presentation. Ensure that the structure of the presentation is explicit, and the sections clearly demarcated and signalled. Use carefully planned visual material and ensure that it is linked with the oral input. Give the child a copy of all visual material and handouts. Slow down the rate of presentation and pause frequently to enable note taking. Repeat and summarise key points. Enable the use of a tape-recorder or laptop computer. Teach note-taking skills and give feedback on the quality of notes taken.

General organisation Allocate time during the day for the organisation of materials. Give specific help on how to take notes, organise files and summarise information.

Comprehension Provide written outlines of chapters to be read, and/or books on tape. Highlight the main ideas and themes in texts. Teach the SQ4R – Stop, Question, Read and Reflect, Recite, (W)rite, and Review and Edit – technique (Markel and Greenbaum, 1996).

Memorisation techniques Encourage the child to accept the need to memorise material. Identify the child's preferred learning style (e.g., auditory, visual, kinaesthetic, combined). Teach memorisation techniques that suit her/his learning style.

Private language Use 'scaffolding' technique to teach the use of 'outer' and 'inner' private speech as a learning strategy.

5. Problem solving

Problem-solving ability is a generic competence that can be applied in a wide range of academic, social and other situations in early and later childhood and adulthood.

Problem-solving activities are particularly relevant to children with AD/HD because they:

- provide a pedagogically rich and motivating context for children with AD/HD to acquire and to maintain their basic knowledge and skills, to develop a sound and accurate understanding of the world, and to generalise their academic and social skills and strategies under conditions which are non-threatening;
- include 'general thinking skills', e.g., being creative, being critical and 'specific strategies', for observing, designing, decision making, team-work, brainstorming, implementing solutions, evaluating outcomes, etc.;
- afford opportunities to use knowledge so as to increase understanding and practise using skills under conditions that are not stressful;
- involve active learning, using relevant practical situations;
- encourage positive attitudes to work and increase motivation for schoolwork;
- require the basic skills and the know-how of everyday life, which can be used to enhance a child's general level of competence, regardless of ability;
- complement the traditional curriculum and enable children to gain better access to it;
- are an exciting and stimulating approach to learning which encourages children to take greater responsibility for their own attainment and educational progress;
- emphasise qualities such as curiosity, resourcefulness, independence, tenacity and patience;
- provide a context for developing organisational and planning skills in creating models of the world (working memory, anticipation of consequences) and testing out these models through first-hand experience (evaluation of outcomes);
- promote growth in self-confidence and self-esteem (Boud and Feletti, 1997; Fisher, 1987; Hanko, 1999; Webster-Stratton, 1999).

Techniques, such as '*I Can Problem Solve*', have been shown to lead to short-term increases in both interpersonal and academic behaviour (Beelman, *et al.*, 1994; Shure, 1994).

General strategies

Problem-solving activities can be integrated into play (Bennett, *et al.*, 1997), Quality Circle Time (Mosley, 1996, 1998, 1999) and basic skills learning (DfEE, 2000b; Fisher, 1987; Robbins, 2000). Note, however, that Quality Circle Time is *not* just an opportunity to meet and exchange news and views. It *is* an activity which should have a purposeful structure, be planned carefully and time-tabled and be monitored on a plan-do-review basis.

Problem-solving process The stages of problem solving are: Define a problem; Ask questions; Brainstorm; Specify and evaluate consequences; Implement action; Evaluate outcomes.

   Children should be taught – using a 'scaffolding' approach – how to: Define a problem – what am I trying to do? Ask questions – what further information can I get? Brainstorm – how many possible solutions can I think of? Specify consequences – what are the possible consequences of each of the solutions? Evaluate consequences – of all the possible solutions, which is best? Implement action – am I achieving the solution as planned? Evaluate outcomes – was I successful in achieving my goal?

Define a problem and ask questions Choose an activity that the child is engaged in during play. Encourage focused attention by asking questions such as, 'Tell me about what you are doing', 'What do you like about this', and asking 'How?' and 'Why?' questions. Here, the focus is on developing a social relationship in order to increase attention span and then cognitive processing. Encourage the manipulation of objects in different ways, so as to foster problem-solving ability. Use Circle Time activities, designed to develop skills and strategies for looking and listening (Mosley, 1996, 1998; Webster-Stratton, 1999).

Brainstorm and specify and evaluate consequences Either during play, Circle Time, or as part of regular teaching activities, for example, Science or Design Technology, encourage children to think of as many ideas as they can, however bizarre, without fear of ridicule. Use Circle Time 'concentration' and 'thinking activities' (Mosley, 1996, 1998; Webster-Stratton, 1999), and encourage older children to record the stages and results of the problem-solving process, as notes and annotated drawings and diagrams. Help children to think of simple cause-effect relationships.

Implement action and evaluate outcomes During play or Circle Time, use role play, puppets and other resources to enact or present in some concrete form different kinds of activity. Encourage children to analyse consequences of action on the basis of direct, first-hand experience. During curriculum-based tasks, use prompts, such as picture cues and solution cards, prepared by the teacher or the child. Help children to identify positive and negative features of a consequence. Encourage them to record evaluations in a written or diagram form. When making evaluative judgements, the child should be encouraged to use self-directed speech, which the teacher should model and 'scaffold'.

Specific strategies

The specific help that the teacher can give is to encourage on-task behaviour, to provide visual or other cues to compensate for working memory deficit, to encourage active participation in role play and in discussions, and to give greater attention to analysing consequences in simple cause-effect relationships. There is evidence (Fletcher, 1999) that children with AD/HD can be very good at thinking of new ideas; what they need is to have the confidence to produce their ideas in a class context.

The development of problem-solving strategies, in both academic and social contexts, has proved a valuable tool in the education of both children and adolescents with AD/HD (Fowler, 1992; Shelton, 1992).

6. Metacognition

'Cognition' is the process by which we come to know about and understand our world. 'Metacognition' is the process by which we come to know what we know, to know what we understand and to know what we can do (Meadows and Cashdan, 1988). As a result of being able to take a 'metacognitive perspective' on ourselves, we are able to monitor and assess what we know, understand and can do, and also what we do not know, do not understand and cannot do. Thus, it enables us, as it were, to see ourselves from 'outside', and thus to analyse and evaluate the appropriateness or the effectiveness of our thinking processes and the effect of our behaviour on ourselves and others. Once we have developed a metacognitive perspective on ourselves, we are able to self-monitor, and thereby to control our own behaviour, that is, develop self-control, which is the long-term goal (Barkley, 1997).

Teaching-learning strategies, particularly those using play, organisational and study skills, and problem-solving, increase children's awareness of the effect of their actions, and their use of hindsight and foresight to predict the outcome of actions, and thus develop their metacognitive competence.

7. Creative subjects

The value of curriculum activities that enable children with emotional and behavioural difficulties has long been recognised (Laslett, 1982). In common with other children with such difficulties, children with AD/HD may experience great difficulty, (a) in analysing their own thoughts and feelings, and anxieties and frustrations, and (b) in expressing them verbally or in writing. Activities that involve the physical manipulation of materials and/or expression of ideas through movement are valuable means for a child to explore and communicate thoughts and ideas. Computer games and other activities may serve the same purpose and may also be commonly chosen activities because of their immediate feedback coupled with stimulating presentation.

Teachers should, therefore, provide as many opportunities as possible for children with AD/HD to choose such activities. With PE, however, there are the twin dangers that their hyperactive and impulsive behaviour may make them a danger to themselves and others, while some children may have co-morbid dyspraxia (Portwood, 2000).

8. Career planning

A serious problem for adolescents is that their difficulties with attention, impulsiveness and hyperactivity tend to overshadow what they have succeeded in achieving, and the potential they have for further success in future. As a result, they may be counselled away from continuing to stay in full-time education in order to take post-16 academic or vocational qualifications (Teeter, 1998). With proper accommodations and differentiated teaching, they can be successful in academic programmes, including medicine and education, or in gaining other vocational qualifications (Richards, 1999).

General and specific strategies

Personal learning planning is a process which begins with children at age 14 years and is aimed at involving adolescents in reviewing and planning their own learning and personal development (Bullock and Wikeley, 1999).

Information Teachers with pastoral responsibilities, in association with careers specialists, can provide information on future qualification and job opportunities. There is the need for careers staff to become aware about both conventional and unconventional vocational qualifications that are appropriate for children with AD/HD (Richards, 1999). Evidence from the USA indicates that with appropriate support, students with AD/HD can benefit from higher education (Teeter, 1998), though autobiographies such as that by Frank (1999) indicate, the quality of support needs to be higher than is the current norm.

Target setting One-to-one discussion between the adolescent and teacher should focus on short- and long-term goals and identify targets for improvement.

Motivation Teachers should use planning sessions to increase student motivation and the self-confidence of students by involving them in planning their own learning and personal development.

Case study 1: Adrian – IEP (extract) (continued)

Principal long-term target:
- *To increase academic attainment through increased focused attention during Literacy and Numeracy Hours.*

Targets (academic):
- *To increase span of time on individual literacy work from approximately one minute (current baseline) to two by end of week two, and six minutes by end of week six, with an emphasis on accuracy;*
- *To encourage writing activities in Design Technology;*
- *To increase number of sums completed per 10-minute session from two (current baseline) to four by end of week two, and 10 by end of week six, with an emphasis on accuracy.*

Targets (interpersonal and behavioural):
- *To apply Behaviour Management Plan, if necessary.*

Targets (self-esteem):
- *To increase Adrian's sense of competence in literacy and numeracy.*

Strategies (academic):
- *Remove all unnecessary materials from desk;*
- *LSA to sit near Adrian during Literacy and Numeracy Hour activities, helping him and two other pupils;*
- *Teacher or LSA to visit Adrian's table frequently to encourage writing.*

Strategies (interpersonal and behavioural):
- *Teacher to sit near Adrian during whole-class Circle Time;*
- *Teacher or LSA to work with small group including Adrian during drama work.*

Strategies (self-esteem):
- *To praise Adrian for work carried out correctly, during or at the end of each lesson;*
- *To review with Adrian his progress at the end of each week.*

Monitoring and assessment:
Adrian's attainment and progress and his behaviour in class will be reviewed by the classteacher, LSA & SENCO each half-term.

Home-school links:
A weekly report is sent to the parents, using the school's proforma.
NOTE. It was decided not to focus on Adrian's organisational skills until he has achieved a greater attention span and fewer careless mistakes, and not to deal with his behaviour, except if it was unacceptable.

Strengths of the IEP include, (i) that it addresses targets in two areas (attainment and self-esteem); (ii) that at least some of the targets include criteria and time scales; (iii) that LSA will not work exclusively with Adrian (which might cause social exclusion); (iv) that there are arrangements for monitoring and assessment, and for communication with the parents.

It could be improved by information about, (i) how stronger home-school links will be established; (ii) whether the parents will be encouraged to build Adrian's self-esteem, based on reports of his attainment at school; (iii) arrangements for monitoring the effect of his medication over time.

CHAPTER 6
Developing interpersonal relationships

Case study 2: David – IEP (extract) (part)

Age 12 years – diagnosed at age eight years as having AD/HD Combined-type, pre-scribed Ritalin – verbal and non-verbal IQ in top 95th percentile, but learning diffi-culties with reading and writing, including fine motor control – initially suspected of having dyslexia (not confirmed) – showed inattentive, impulsive and aggressive behaviour in class, at lunchtime and at home, e.g., maximum attention span in most curriculum subjects was three minutes unless directly supervised, climbing on fur-niture, running around excessively, hardly ever standing still, only ever slept for four hours a night.

Current areas of concern: although David's attention has improved greatly, he still requires LSA support in all academic lessons, where he is still impulsive (e.g., blurt-ing out answers), and is frequently verbally abusive and unwilling to do as he is told; his attainment level is broadly in line with that of his peers (range L3-L5).

Strengths: David responds well to praise, is able to self-monitor and record behaviour on star chart, and talks about how to behave in order to gain praise; very supportive parents.

The information given is valuable in that it records: (i) information about previous and current symptoms; (ii) performance on standardised tests; (iii) a differential diagnosis, which excludes dyslexia; (iv) teacher behaviour (praise) to which he responds positively; and (v) attitude of parents. There are, however, no details about: (i) Ritalin (dosage, frequency, whether monitored); (ii) factors which tend to precipitate David's abusive and confrontational behaviour; (iii) level of attainment in different curriculum areas, including areas of curriculum strength (if any).

The development of social relationships involves understanding another person's inter-pretation of behaviour and events and responding appropriately. Within the inclusive classroom, this involves developing: (i) appropriate work-related behaviour; and (ii) good relationships with peers in day-to-day classroom, lunchtime and playground activities, and after school homework and recreation (DfEE/QCA, 1999). The teacher's and parents' role is to enable children to develop this competence, at school and in daily life.

Principles and practice

Two different but complementary approaches have been developed – a '*behavioural*' approach, and a '*cognitive-metacognitive*' approach. With the first, the goal is to enable the child to respond appropriately in interpersonal and other situations by controlling her/his behaviour. Attempts are made, (a) to alter aspects of the child's environment (the *antecedents* to any behaviour) so that the range of choices is limited, (b) to modify the child's response to situations (the *behaviour*), by (c) giving positive reinforcement (rewards) to desired or acceptable behaviours, and negative reinforcement (withholding rewards or punishment) to undesired or unacceptable behaviours (the *consequences*). In essence, the behavioural approach seeks to *control the child's behaviour from outside*, with the child being treated as a more or less 'non-thinking' individual. In many situations, this is accompanied by talking to the child about the reasons why certain behaviours are acceptable while others are not. Such explanations mark the beginning of the 'cognitive-metacognitive' approach, since the child is being encouraged to make sense of her/his own actions and their consequences.

The 'cognitive-metacognitive' approach seeks to encourage the child to think about her/his behaviour and its effect on others. The emphasis is upon developing the child's understanding of, for example, the reasons behind the classroom rules (cognition), and encouraging reflection on her/his own actions and their effect on others (metacognition). The goal is *self-control*. The two approaches are complementary in that teachers and parents begin by imposing control and gradually educate the child toward self-control, and in that when the child fails to exercise self-control, external control can be imposed.

Through the eyes of the child

It is valuable, first, to reflect on the world though the eyes of a child with AD/HD (Goldstein and Goldstein, 1990). This helps the teacher and parent to understand a child's often very difficult and frequently annoying behaviour in class and at home. It is important to bear in mind:

1. that their inappropriate behaviour is more or less transitory – for much of the time, their behaviour is indistinguishable from that of their peers;
2. that it is situation specific – it occurs only in certain situations or under certain conditions;
3. that certain aspects of their behaviour may partly be learnt – butting in on conversations or delinquent behaviour leads to a measure of success, at least in the short term;
4. that many aspects of their behaviour are quantitatively rather than qualitatively

different from that of other children – each child in the class is somewhere along the continua of inattention, impulsiveness and hyperactivity, and the associated behaviours;

5. that the child's behaviour is logical from her/his point of view – given the way that s/he is, and the extent to which inappropriate behaviour may have been rewarded in the past, s/he acts in ways which seem sensible at the time;

6. that her/his behaviour can be understood as a strategy – albeit a maladaptive one – for coping with the world (Laslett, 1982).

It is important also to distinguish between non-compliance and incompetence (Goldstein and Goldstein, 1990). This is most obviously the case among younger children with AD/HD, whose behaviour may be indistinguishable from that of their non- AD/HD peers.

Behavioural approach

1. Antecedents

There are two kinds of antecedents, those which *predispose* a child to act in a certain kind of way and those which *precipitate* a particular behaviour. Predisposing antecedents develop as the result of interaction between 'within-child' characteristics, and the learning environment (Alban-Metcalfe, 1998). Children with AD/HD are predisposed to act in ways that range from being anti-social to being shy and withdrawn. However, whether a child responds in any of these ways on a given occasion depends on internal and external factors that precipitate a particular behaviour. For example, whether or not an activity is interesting and stimulating, whether there are other competing stimuli, whether a task is proving to be difficult to achieve and therefore frustrating, whether or not the teacher or another adult is taking an interest.

General and specific strategies

The strategies described here are equally applicable to all children (Barkley, 1998; Cooper, 1999; Cooper and Ideus, 1996; DuPaul and Stoner, 1994; Hanko, 1999; Robin, 1998; Teeter, 1998; Webster-Stratton, 1999).

(a) Predisposing antecedents

Beliefs and expectations Children should be encouraged to believe that school work is relevant. Teachers should communicate high expectations of success. Activities should be meaningful and emphasise active pupil involvement (Teeter and Stewart, 1997).

Organisation Younger children should be provided with a variety of closely monitored educational experiences, including self-paced and other-paced activities. Work should be divided into well-defined, predictable and timed chunks. Noise levels should be low when new tasks are being learnt.

(b) Precipitating antecedents

Information The class teacher and all other staff must be fully informed about the nature of AD/HD, and the range of teaching and behaviour management strategies available.

Planning A 'Behaviour Management Plan' should be devised which anticipates the range of likely pupil responses, and specifies the *hierarchy* of different actions that can be taken, proactively and reactively, to prevent, discourage or respond to disruptive behaviour.

Communication The Plan should be communicated to all staff and others who work in the school.

Identifying positive targets A major goal is the promotion of positive behaviours, such as listening to what other children have to say, sharing, taking turns, sitting quietly. These can involve, (a) demonstration and modelling by the teacher and other children of prosocial behaviour; and (b) behaviours that require action, rather than inaction – consistent with Lindsley's 'dead man' principle (Lindsey, 1991), children should be rewarded for doing something, rather than not doing something. Intervention that seeks the elimination of 'negative' behaviours, is only half the story.

Setting achievable targets Just as with academic tasks, behavioural targets should be small in number, well defined and achievable. Behavioural targets should take into account both the chronological age of the child (which can act as a rough guide to what can be expected) and her/his developmental age. When identifying target behaviours, it is important to distinguish between those which are 'high priority' in that, for example, they disrupt other children's learning, such as blurting out answers before other children have had a chance to speak, constantly interrupting when another child is answering a question or disturbing other children during individual work, and those that do not have a disruptive effect. Examples of the latter would be continually fidgeting, or daydreaming every now and then, neither of which interferes with ongoing class activities. This is not to say that such behaviours should never be tackled; rather, it is a question of when – and also how.

Setting specific targets Targets such as, 'If you sit near me, with your hands on your knees during story time, then ... [specified reward]', or 'Each time you put your hand up without calling out the answer, then ... [specified reward]' describe the actions asked of the child in a precise and positive way. In contrast, to say, 'If you are good during Circle Time, you can have a star for your star chart' is unlikely to change the behaviour of a child who spends much of Circle Time poking other children and shouting out answers.

Making small steps Observe the child over a five-minute period, to establish a behavioural 'baseline'. For a Year 1 child, a target such as 'listening attentively' (which implies no interruptions) for two minutes might be achievable, and would address both hyperactivity and impulsiveness. It is likely that progress will be slow, but once achieved, the length of time to be rewarded can be extended gradually. For severe problems among older children, for example, little or no compliance or work completion, reinforcement targets should be set at levels that mean the child can receive credit for small successes. For a child who frequently blurts out answers, the reward could be for doing so only twice during a session, or for a child with a low work completion rate, completing four out of 10 sums in mathematics. Once success has been achieved, the expectations can be raised. The most common reasons why behaviour management techniques fail are setting unachievable expectations and setting expectations that are outside the child's behaviour repertoire. Tasks can gradually be made more challenging, either by increasing the difficulty of the task itself, e.g., a longer period on-task, more sums to be completed, or by increasing the complexity of the task, e.g., sitting quietly and putting up a 'quiet' hand before receiving a reward.

Number of targets set The principles governing how many targets are set should take account of, (a) frequency of occurrence – if the behaviour occurs frequently, the teacher will be fully occupied monitoring it; (b) child's developmental age – for younger children, one or two targets will be the limit of their understanding and memory, older children understand and remember more and can cope with more complex reward programmes; (c) availability of dedicated adult time – the teacher can set more targets if much of the child's behaviour is being monitored by the teacher or LSA, or other adult.

Distractor activities Allow a child who is impulsive or hyperactive to hold a favourite object in their hand during Circle Time, or doodle or draw sketches during story time, to enable them to remain on-task and not disrupt the lesson.

Wriggle zone Provide a wriggle zone, which a child can use to expend their bottled-up energy without interfering with what their peers are doing. At first, suggest when the child goes to the wriggle zone for a few minutes. With time, the child should be encouraged to make the decision for her/himself – the beginning of self-control.

Rules A maximum of three rules should be set. These should be explained to the child and should be displayed prominently, both in a written form and as drawings or diagrams.

Managing transitions Instructions should be clear and unambiguous and coupled with the preparation in advance of a number of high-quality, well-resourced tasks which will stimulate the interest of the child. The presence of a teacher/LSA during transitions periods can be valuable.

Peer mediation Peers in general, or a particular 'buddy', can provide appropriate role models and can also serve to establish learning conditions – particularly pair or small group work – which are conducive to on-task behaviour. It may be appropriate to discuss the nature of AD/HD with the class, or with selected groups of pupils.

Remove distractors As noted above, the removal of distractors is an essential pre-requisite for on-task behaviour.

2. Behaviour

The principal ways in which the behaviour of children with AD/HD is different from that of other children is that it may sometimes be more extreme, particularly when co-morbidly associated with Conduct Disorder or Oppositional Defiant Disorder.

General strategies

Observation and record keeping Particularly during the first part of a new year or new term, the teacher will need information about the children's behaviour which is, (a) specific, objective and behaviourally based (as distinct from vague, subjective and impressionistic), and (b) both criterion- and ipsative-referenced. Criterion referencing involves making judgements against pre-determined criteria, such as, what one might expect of a 4–5, a 10–11, or a 14–15 year old boy or girl. Ipsative referencing involves making comparisons between what a child did or achieved on occasion A, and what the same child did on occasion B, some time later. Both provide evidence of progress, which can be shared with the child her/himself.

Consistency and predictability For all pupils, consistency and predictability both of teacher behaviour, for example, when challenged by a pupil, and in her/his expectations of how pupils should behave, are essential. This is particularly the case for children with AD/HD, owing to their difficulty with foresight and hindsight.

Specific strategy

Proximity One of the strongest motivators for children with AD/HD is the proximity of an adult who shows an interest in what they are doing. For some, sitting near the teacher during Circle Time and working in close proximity to an adult and getting frequent attention is enough. Others need almost constant attention and/or close proximity to an LSA.

3. Consequences

It is possible to distinguish different kinds of consequences – *involuntary* and *voluntary*. An involuntary consequence of a confrontation with the teacher may be that, immediately afterwards, a pupil will be unable to concentrate on their work. Within the voluntary category two further distinctions can be made: (a) *intended*, as when the teacher deliberately sets out to reinforce (reward or punish) a certain behaviour; and (b) *unintended*, as when s/he continues to respond to a child's misbehaviour, thereby (unintentionally) rewarding the child by giving teacher attention. Teachers have, therefore, to monitor their own behaviour to ensure that they are not giving the wrong message.

(a) Avoiding unintended reinforcement
General and specific strategies

Behaviour to ignore The Behaviour Management Plan must specify which behaviours can and which behaviours cannot be ignored. The criteria for deciding what to ignore are: (i) whether the behaviour is potentially dangerous to the child or to others in the class; (ii) whether the behaviour interferes with the learning process. Behaviours over which the child has little or no control, such as a hyperactive child fidgeting with objects or wriggling on the chair, should be ignored even though they can be a source of irritation. Actions which do not have a major disruptive influence can often be eliminated by consistent application of a strategy of ignoring.

How to ignore The action of ignoring is not itself a source of reinforcement. However, if coupled with, say, glaring at the child, or making sarcastic remarks, it conveys the message that the teacher is still giving the child attention and is thus rewarding. Conversely, avoiding eye contact or even walking away and attending to another child, can be effective. It is likely, however, that the behaviour will get worse – perhaps much worse – before it gets better. Persistence, even over a 10-minute period, may be needed. As soon as a child starts to act in a desired way, her/his behaviour should be the subject of an immediate reward.

Distractors Ignoring one behaviour can be accompanied by re-directing attention to a different task. Simply to prevent the child from participating in one activity would be inconsistent with the 'dead man' principle.

(b) Giving intended reinforcement

General strategies

Noticing good behaviour A key to success is to catch children being good, since it serves both as a reward and a model for future behaviour. It is particularly important immediately following a period of ignoring inappropriate behaviour.

Recording good behaviour: charts A chart for a child who is impulsive can record how often a desired behaviour is achieved. For example, a 'Quiet Hand Chart', would comprise a picture of the desired behaviour and a grid showing the days of the week and the different sessions within the day. After establishing a baseline, the teacher and pupil would jointly agree a target for each session, and the reward for success.

Recording good behaviour: thermometer Actions, such as disturbing a fellow pupil, are recorded as they occur by the pupil and/or teacher. At the end of the session, the total number (hopefully less than a previously agreed target) is discussed with the child, and may lead to a reward. Involving the child in recording is the beginning of a cognitive-metacognitive approach.

Redirecting behaviour Where possible, non-verbal signals should be used to indicate that an action is inappropriate, for example, by pointing to class rules – or to special rules for that particular child. Non-verbal signals have the advantage that they do not draw the child's behaviour to the notice of the whole class.

Managing misbehaviour The ultimate way of managing misbehaviour is 'Time out', but before the teacher gets to that stage, a hierarchy of other actions is available. In all cases, the principles are that negative consequences should be: applied immediately and consistently; convenient to enforce; recognised by the child as a choice that s/he has made; non-punitive; behaviour-related. For children with AD/HD, the expected behaviour must be achievable, especially in the case of younger ones, and the management should tend to encourage self-control. Therefore, consequences should, (a) be logical, and (b) be discussed in advance with the child – dangerous use of scissors will result in them being taken away, if you don't complete your work you will have to stay in at break time.

Response cost Usually positive comments and rewards on their own are not enough to reduce oppositional behaviour. Response cost is a generic term applied to situations in which some kind of negative reinforcement becomes a consequence of inappropriate behaviour by the child. The degree of severity of the negative reinforcement can vary greatly but – particularly with children with AD/HD – should be under conditions in which the amount of positive reinforcement vastly exceeds the negative. To achieve this, the teacher may have to ignore much inappropriate behaviour.

Aggressive, disruptive and non-compliant behaviour can be targeted by recording behaviour at 30-minute intervals, using colour codes – green (good), yellow (initial non-compliance), blue (repeated non-compliance), red (unacceptable behaviour) – coupled with verbal feedback and one of four reinforcers. The reinforcers are: a Reward for green, a Reprimand for yellow, a Doing Task for blue, or Time Out for red.

Reprimands Provided that they are brief and directed at an individual child, and are delivered in a way that is calm, firm and consistent, reprimands can be more effective than praise on its own for some persistent problems. However, reprimands which are given late and/or inconsistently or which are non-specific are ineffective, and may even lead to increased disruption.

Doing Tasks Here, pupils are given additional tasks that they have to complete before they are allowed out at break time, or are allowed to participate in a chosen activity. A certain area of the room may be set aside for carrying out these tasks.

Time out This is the ultimate sanction available to the teacher. The factors to bear in mind include: location – somewhere away from other children, under adult supervision, perhaps in another classroom; length of time out – three minutes for younger children, more for older ones, including two minutes of good behaviour; hierarchy of behaviours – use only for serious acts, such as aggressiveness, consistent non-compliance or defiance.

Specific strategies

Habituation A real danger, particularly among children with AD/HD, is that the child becomes used, or 'habituated', to the particular reinforcement. When this happens, positive and negative reinforcements are no longer effective.

Choice of reinforcer Because of rapid habituation, it is important, (a) to establish – either from observation or discussion – the *range* of activities a particular child finds rewarding (or a punishment), and (b) to be sensitive to any change in effectiveness. Many children with AD/HD regard a chance to work on a computer rewarding, but the teacher should try to establish which social activities the child enjoys, such as helping the teacher.

Token systems Tokens can be earned, contingent on behaviour such as remaining on-task or being compliant over agreed periods of time. These can then be exchanged for gaining special privileges, free time, tangible rewards, etc. Children with AD/HD are, however, poor at generalising what they learn to other situations, and thus there is the need to persist with using a token economy over a long period of time (Stokes and Osnes, 1989). A 'Response cost' version of this system can be used with older pupils, such that tokens can be given or taken away, as appropriate.

Contingency contracting As with token economies, contractual agreements specify desired attainment and behaviour, and consequences (both positive and negative) contingent on performance. The consequences should be preferred activities, privileges or other rewards, rather than secondary reinforcers, such as tokens or gold stars. Immediate, primary rewards are appropriate because, since some tasks may take a long time to complete, there may already be a long delay between the initial behaviour and the rein-forcement. Contingency contracting is not suitable for pupils below age six years, since it is only effective with pupils who have the ability to develop rules based on experience, and to defer reinforcement for longer periods of time. The proposed length of delay should be considered carefully. Thus, for example, to achieve 80 per cent success on an academic task for five days running would be too difficult for a pupil of eight years. Greater success is likely if contracts extend over the period of a day or half a day, and at first a small number of small targets should be set; the standards for success should not be too high and the task should comprise only a small number of steps. Once a pupil has experienced success, the number of steps can be increased, the standards raised and the task can be made more complex.

Positive versus negative reinforcement Positive reinforcement, such as praise and teacher atten-tion, in isolation, does not produce systematic and consistent changes in the classroom behaviour of children with AD/HD. Indeed, positive reinforcement without prudent negative reinforcement may actually lead to a decrease in on-task behaviour and work productivity. Most effective is negative reinforcement in a positive reinforcement-rich environment (Pfiffer and Barkley, 1990). The ratio of positive to negative should be at least 2:1 (Teeter, 1998). Carlson (1997) found that use of response costs technique(s) led to a decrease in motivation, while positive reinforcement increased it. If the goal is to lead the child to be intrinsically motivated, long-term success is likely to be associated with positive aspects of reinforcement.

Cognitive-metacognitive approach

In this approach, which is sometimes referred to as 'cognitive-behavioural', the emphasis is on enabling the child to have control over her/his actions. The goal, then, is to encourage and enable responsibility and independence. This approach has, therefore, become popular for treating classroom behaviour associated with AD/HD (Shapiro and Cole, 1994). The techniques and strategies used are attractive because they are easy to use, certainly in comparison with behaviourally based management schedules. However, they only start to become effective when the child has reached a certain level of cognitive-metacognitive and dispositional maturity. In practical terms, this means during middle-late childhood and adolescence. This is not to say that they should not be used earlier. Indeed, one of the goals of play among young children is to enable them to develop a meta-cognitive perspective. Children with AD/HD are slower to achieve this perspective.

Typically, the strategies and techniques comprise combinations of self-monitoring, self-reinforcement, and/or self-instruction (Barkley, 1998; DuPaul and Stoner, 1994; Teeter, 1998; Webster-Stratton, 1999).

General and specific strategies

Strategies for encouraging and enabling children with AD/HD to develop a cognitive-metacognitive perspective on their actions, and their effect on others, are the same as for other children. The only difference is that the development of children with AD/HD is delayed.

Self-monitoring The objective is for the child to be able to observe and to record her/his own behaviour. The child is taught to recognise instances of when they are on-task during academic work, and to record this, for example, with the teacher indicating at regular intervals, either personally or using an electronic device that emits an auditory or visual signal, when the child should self-monitor. The child then determines and records whether or not s/he was on-task.

Self-monitoring can be used in isolation, but is more often used in combination with other self-management techniques. The evidence suggests that it is effective in increasing on-task behaviour, particularly in combination with self-reinforcement or reinforcement by others, though it has not been studied extensively among children with a clinical diagnosis of AD/HD (DuPaul and Stoner, 1994).

Self-reinforcement This involves the child both monitoring and evaluating her/his own performance and behaviour. The additional self-reinforcement dimension encourages and enables the child not merely to record their own behaviour, but also to make judgements about it – in other words, to begin to take charge of their life. The teaching of self-reinforcement follows the traditional Vygotskian 'scaffolding' model (Vygotsky, 1978). In the case of behaviour management, however, the process is slightly more complicated in that the process of increasing self-reinforcement occurs in parallel with a corresponding decrease in the use of externally based (extrinsic) behaviour management techniques. As self-reinforcement increases, so is it possible for external reinforcement to decrease without a deterioration in behaviour. It is important to bear in mind, however, that both the increase in self-reinforcement and the decrease in external reinforcement, will take place over a very long period of time, with inevitable 'relapses'.

The use of self-monitoring and self-reinforcement techniques is particularly appropriate with older children and adolescents. This is partly because they provide a more acceptable, more 'dignified', form of intervention, and partly because, as they mature cognitively and emotionally, older children become potentially more capable of self-regulation. Significant improvements in behaviour have been maintained with different activities in mainstream classrooms (Smith *et al.*, 1992). The only point of caution is that the effectiveness of the intervention depends on the continued use of external reinforcements until quite late in the programme. A combination of self-monitoring and self-evaluation has been shown to be effective in increasing on-task behaviour, accuracy on academic tasks and peer relations, especially in combination with medication (Barkley, 1989; DuPaul and Stoner, 1994).

Self-instruction The principle behind self-instruction is also derived from the work of Vygotsky and builds on the observation that children with AD/HD do use self-directed talk, but do not do so as effectively as other children. Self-talk acts in such a way as to organise and to control behaviour, and can be taught using 'scaffolding' – verbal commentary and modelling by teacher; teacher and child both comment on the child's actions, and how they could be more effective; teacher input fades and the child provides most of the commentary, initially out loud and later whispering; only the child gives the verbal commentary, still out loud; child continues to talk about what s/he is doing, but no longer out loud, i.e., s/he progresses to the 'inner speech' stage. The significance of inner speech is that it serves the same self-regulatory purpose in interpersonal as in academic contexts.

In spite of its intuitive appeal, when taught is isolation, self-regulation has not always been successful with children with AD/HD (Barkley, 1989). It has, however, been found to be effective when used in combination with other interventions, e.g., contingent management, stimulant medication, with hyperactive children (Braswell and Bloomquist,

1991). The reasons why self-instruction was not effective are twofold. One, is that although the strategy was predicated on the belief that it would lead to generalisation from one context to another, generalisation has not been evident (Barkley, 1989). Two, is the question as to what the within-child changes are. The assumption was that they would be cognitive; it may be that they are, in fact, motivational, in which case the training may be effective for the same reasons as teacher-controlled behaviour management – the reward of intensive teacher attention.

It is the case, however, that many older adolescents and adults with AD/HD do use inner speech and self-instruction to control their behaviour in academic and social contexts. The question that teachers and others need to address is why, when two other cognitive-metacognitive strategies – self-monitoring and self-evaluation – can be effective with children and adolescents of school age, currently used self-instruction techniques are not. One strongly contending possibility is the context in which self-instruction techniques are taught, and hence their meaningfulness to the child. It is a well-established educational principle that the most effective learning occurs when the content has personal significance to the learner (Rogers, 1961). One such context is social problem solving.

Problem solving The value of teaching problem solving in academic contexts (Chapter 5), is matched by its use in the context of social interaction, which can be taught effectively during Quality Circle Time or dedicated Personal and Social Education lessons. Children should be encouraged:

- to pay attention to, and to express, their feelings – 'I feel angry because other children won't let me play with them', and the feelings of others;
- to generate solutions or choices – 'Suppose another child started hitting you. What would you do?', a situation where puppets and role play can be used to great effect;
- to use imagination and think of 'What if ...' situations, again using puppets and role play, and also cues to help their working memory;
- to think about the consequences of their own role play (or their puppets') actions, and to think about and to practise how they will act if they are unhappy with the consequences;
- to think of how the hypothetical solutions that have been explored can be applied in their own lives, with intensive one-to-one support from an adult, and perhaps a more mature classmate who can model and guide appropriate pro-social behaviour;
- to evaluate real life situations, in relation to questions about safety, fairness and feelings that are relevant, with prompts from the adult to enable accurate remembering of past events (Webster-Stratton, 1999).

Case study 2: David – IEP (extract) (continued)

Principal long-term target:
- To increase academic attainment in English;
- To develop interpersonal relationships, in particular behaviour in class.

Targets (academic) – English:
- To continue to increase focused attention and organisation when writing stories and poems;
- To continue to take more care with handwriting (slow down, check letter formation and spelling).

N.B. David has different academic targets for each curriculum area.

Targets (interpersonal and behavioural):
- To continue to encourage David to monitor his own behaviour and to record using star chart;
- To reduce David's abusive and confrontational behaviour, starting with eight occasions per day as a baseline, and aiming for four occasions per day within six weeks;

Targets (self-esteem):
- To increase David's sense of competence in literacy.

Strategies (academic):
- LSA to sit near David during Literacy activities, helping him and two other pupils;
- Teacher or LSA to visit David's table frequently to encourage writing.

Strategies (interpersonal and behavioural):
- LSA for English to sit near and help David focus attention and to control blurting out during lessons;
- Teacher to sit near David during whole-class Circle Time activities;
- Teacher or LSA to work with small group including David during drama work;
- To continue prediction activities which consider the effects of actions (e.g., verbal abuse, fighting) on others, during drama and Circle Time;
- To introduce a 'thermometer' for David to record (by taking away points) his abusive or confrontational behaviour;
- For David to discuss with his form teacher his success each evening after school;
- To continue to implement the Behaviour Management Plan, as required;

Strategies (self-esteem):
- To praise David for work carried out correctly, during or at the end of each lesson;
- To review with David his progress at the end of each week;
- To communicate successes to parents on weekly basis.

Monitoring and assessment:
David's attainment and progress and his behaviour in class will be reviewed by the class teacher, LSA and SENCO each half-term.

Home-school links:
A weekly report is sent to the parents, using the school's proforma.

Strengths of the IEP include: (i) that it addresses targets in all three areas; (ii) that at least some of the targets include criteria and time scales; (iii) that LSA is not targeted exclusively on David (which might cause social exclusion); (iv) that there are arrangements for monitoring and assessment and for communication with the parents.

It could be improved by information about: (i) how different aspects of David's inattentiveness are being addressed; (ii) strategies for building on his strengths; (iii) arrangements for monitoring the effect of his medication over time.

CHAPTER 7

Enhancing self-esteem

Case study 3: Harriet – IEP (extract) (first part)
Age 10 years – diagnosed at age 9 years as having AD/HD Inattentive-type, and with two symptoms of hyperactivity – considered for some time to be of low ability because of consistently low level of attainment – when tested at age 9 she was found to have average scores on verbal and non-verbal reasoning tests – has always been very shy and uncommunicative.

Current areas of concern: short attention span; easily distractible; tends to grab and fiddle with any nearby objects; does not seem to listen or follow instructions; needs constant help with organising her work, e.g., writing a story; fidgets a lot with hands, if no object available; often leaves her seat in class; low level of academic attainment: L1-L2 in core and foundation subjects, except Art L4; self-esteem: does not appear proud of her work; does not seek to join a group, and is rarely chosen by others.

Strengths: very good at Art, and model making in Design Technology; mother regularly attends parents' evenings.

The information given is valuable in that it records: (i) details of her inattentive behaviour, and two aspects of hyperactivity; (ii) evidence from standardised tests that an earlier diagnosis of low ability was incorrect; (iii) evidence to suggest that she has low self-esteem; (iv) some areas of strength. There is no evidence to suggest that either parent has been directly involved in intervention.

Principles and practice

There is clear evidence that level of achievement is affected by how the child feels about her/himself, such that self-esteem is positively correlated with achievement (Burns, 1982; Lawrence, 1996). It has also been found that low self-esteem is a characteristic of children with emotional and behavioural problems (DFE, 1994). It is also true that teachers and parents are in a powerful position to affect children's self-esteem. They do so partly through the kind of activities that the child is encouraged and enabled to participate in – which can lead to increased *competence* – and partly through developing a caring relationship with the child – which can lead to increased *confidence*. Indeed, the interaction between competence and confidence is central to our understanding of how to enhance self-esteem.

Self-esteem is one of a number of terms commonly used in relation to self, often without precise definition. The relationship between self-esteem and other self-referent terms can be represented as follows:

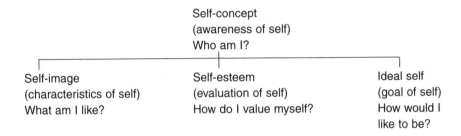

The answer to the, 'Who am I?' question is a summary of how I see myself. It comprises certain aspects of me that are 'central' to me being me – those aspects which, if changed, would mean that I would no longer be me – such as my core values, plus certain aspects which are more or less peripheral – such as what I look like, how clever I am, how many friends I have. Children (and adults) tend to answer the 'What am I like?' and 'How do I value myself?' questions in relation to six main dimensions: physical appearance, academic attainment, behaviour, popularity, happiness, anxiety. In order to understand how this occurs, Charles Cooley (1902) coined the phrase 'looking glass self'. If we want to know about our physical appearance, we look at our reflection in a mirror; if we want to know what we are like as a person, we use the behaviour of others towards us as the reflection. If others treat us as being attractive, clever, fun to be with, etc., this is the image we have of ourselves. And since being attractive, clever and fun to be with are attributes that are evaluated highly in our society, then this image of ourselves leads us to have high self-esteem.

Our ideal self corresponds to what we would like to be like, what we strive to achieve. If our ideal self and our self-image were identical, we might tend to be apathetic and complacent. So, a discrepancy between our self-image and our ideal self can lead us to be motivated to succeed at different tasks, so that we can achieve goals; a manageable discrepancy is, therefore, healthy in promoting development. However, a discrepancy which is so great as to be unmanageable will tend to be debilitating, and may lead to a sense of 'learned helplessness'. As far as self-esteem is concerned, the greater the discrepancy the lower the self-esteem.

Significant others

For pupils, perhaps the greatest influences on their self-image and self-esteem (and on their ideal self) are their teacher, their parents and their peers – people that are described as 'significant others'. Teachers' communicate their satisfaction or dissatisfaction, their approval or disapproval, their anxiety or contentment and so on, to pupils in a variety of ways. Most communication is intentional, but some communication occurs unintentionally – sometimes through the occasional 'throw away' word, sometimes through the values that are implicit in how judgements are made. An example of giving unintended message would be, 'Please fetch the Register, James, you're always reliable', which is only likely to make James feel good! School or teacher values are evident where there is emphasis on competition rather than cooperation. A further aspect of school life is that whereas adults are able to maintain their self-esteem by avoiding tasks at which they are likely to fail – crossword puzzles in the case of one of the authors – pupils may have learning tasks at which they will fail imposed on them.

Vicious and virtuous circles

As indicated above, confidence and competence are two important concepts in the development of self-esteem. Having confidence – as tennis players at Wimbledon demonstrate annually – leads to competence, measured in terms of successful shots and winning games. Success (competence), in turn, leads the player to become more confident, to the point where they try out more daring shots, which leads to more success, and so what might be described as a 'virtuous' circle continues.

This kind of analysis can be applied to pupils with AD/HD, but with the strong possibility that what will develop will be a 'vicious' circle that can only be changed into a 'virtuous' cycle with expert help and guidance (see Figures 7.1a and 7.1b).

The two figures serve to summarise some of the difficulties that any child can experience, and to put into context some of the strategies for promoting teaching and learning and behaviour management described in Chapters 5 and 6. The focus is on curriculum planning and delivery, designed to lead, through experiences of success, to a feeling of *competence*, coupled with a class and school ethos that, through valuing all pupils and recognising their achievements, leads to a feeling of *confidence*. Failure to devise and deliver an appropriate IEP, with specified targets and techniques, is likely to lead to lack of competence. Failure to develop and foster an ethos and specific teacher actions that recognise and value pupils and what they achieve, and the promotion of competition between pupils, are likely to lead to a lack of *confidence*.

Conversely, informed and pedagogically sound curricula and teaching methods can lead to increased competence, while an ethos and teacher actions that recognise and value

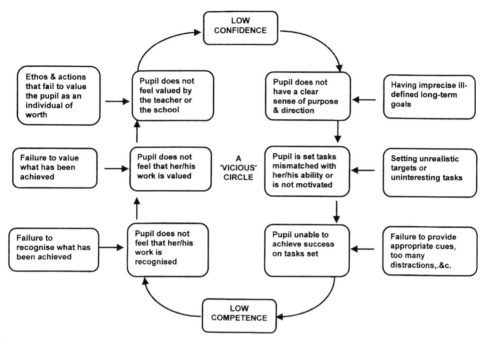

Figure 7.1a: A vicious circle

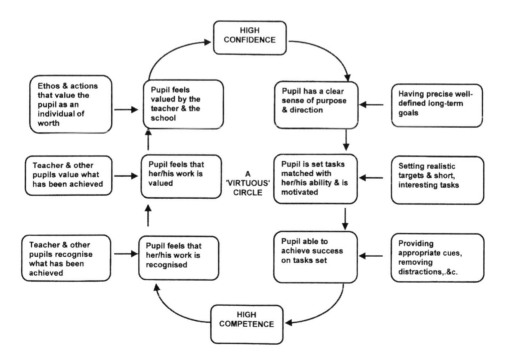

Figure 7.1b: A virtuous circle

pupils and their achievements and encouragement of cooperation, are likely to enhance confidence. It is, however, essential that: (i) pupils must experience *real* success on *valued* tasks; and (ii) any praise or positive comments made must be *genuine* – all aspects of the teacher's behaviour must be authentic!

Effects of failure on self-esteem

While the emphasis on teaching should be on enhancing self-esteem, particularly among children with AD/HD, teachers should be aware of the possible consequences of pupils' previous learning experiences. One, is that, depending on other dispositional characteristics, a pupil will respond to a difficult situation either by avoiding it or by appearing to be arrogant and boastful. Both of these are responses of pupils with low self-esteem. A second, is in terms of motivation. A pupil with low self-esteem may regard certain academic or social activities as 'too difficult' for them, with the result that they do not even begin the tackle them. Third, is that low self-esteem can lead a pupil to be highly resistant to change. Doing things the same way each time can lead to a sense of security; trying new ways of approaching things carries with it the risk of failure, with the consequence of threatening an already low self-concept (Lawrence, 1996).

Defence mechanisms

Although having low self-esteem is not a desirable state to be in, for some pupils it is a state in which they feel comfortable. This is because they have become used to thinking poorly of themselves, and used to having others hold them in low regard, which in turn enables them to predict their own responses to situations and to predict how others will treat them. They know, for example, that if they tackle certain kinds of tasks they will fail; they know that when they fail, others will laugh at them or show disrespect in some other way. Thus, paradoxically, having a measure of 'predictive control' over themselves and their environment serves to give a certain sense of security.

This means that, when the teacher sets a task at a level at which they can and do succeed, or when the teacher genuinely praises them for something that they have done well, they may respond by using one of two defence mechanisms – denial or distortion. Denial may take the form of saying, 'This isn't my work', and even tearing up their work. Alternatively, the pupil might distort the situation by saying, for example, 'I succeeded because the teacher gave me so much help – it's her work, not mine'. It can be less stressful for such pupils – whose personal perceptions of themselves are already likely to be in turmoil – to disown any new and different way of seeing themselves, than to perceive themselves in a new, more favourable light. The pupil, consciously or unconsciously, regards a change in self-perception as a source of further uncertainty or confusion.

General and specific strategy

The same kinds of approach are appropriate for enhancing the self-esteem of all children. The only difference among those with AD/HD is that previous and continuing experiences of failure in both academic and social situations may have resulted in very low self-esteem.

Quality Circle Time Self-esteem can be enhanced directly through encouraging pupils to analyse and to talk about their thoughts, feelings and beliefs, and to make complimentary comments about each others' work and achievements. An example of this is an activity in which, with the whole class seated in a circle, pupil A throws a bean bag to pupil B, and then says to pupil B, 'I like you because ...'. Initially the first pupil may focus on physical characteristics, such as, 'I like you because you've got curly hair', but gradually the reasons progress to personality attributes and behaviours, e.g., 'I like you because you're kind to others'. With the establishment of ground rules that include a prohibition of any negative remarks, the potential of this and other techniques is to have beneficial effects on self-esteem and social competence (e.g., Mosley, 1996, 1998; Webster-Stratton, 1999).

Circle Time activities can also have an indirect effect on enhancing self-esteem through academic tasks. These can range from increasing 'low level' academic competences, such as active listening or sequencing, to 'high level' competences, such as problem solving (Mosley, 1996, 1998). The particular significance for Circle Time activities, as compared to individual work, for pupils with a low self-esteem is that their achievements are witnessed by the whole class, which has implications for how the pupil evaluates or re-evaluates her/himself and for how s/he is evaluated and re-evaluated by classmates, with implications for an increased range of future interactions.

Indirect effects of social relations-focused activities can be equally beneficial. Such activities can range from Talking about friendship, through Resolving conflict, to Dealing with bullying, gender issues and racism (Mosley, 1996, 1998; Webster-Stratton, 1999). It is important to bear in mind that although Circle Time tends to be associated in people's minds with younger pupils, when the emphasis is on problem-solving behaviour or discussing moral values, it can be equally valuable up to Key Stage 4. Indeed, Mosley (1998) gives examples of ways in which it can be a very effective technique in teachers' professional development.

Teacher responses to difficult situations

Teachers with high self-esteem are generally more able to deal with pupils with severe behavioural problems, since they tend not to be threatened by such behaviour and to be able to accept rather than reject the pupil. Because such pupils impinge on teachers in what can often be an unpleasant way, there is the danger that the teacher will deal with the behaviour in such a way that will lead to a reduction in the pupil's self-esteem, with a consequent deterioration of teacher-pupil relations and an escalation of the problem. What is important, therefore, is for teachers to interact with pupils at all times, including when imposing discipline, in ways that enhance, or are at least neutral to, the pupils' self-esteem. The key to maintaining a quality teacher-pupil relationship is a focus on empathising with but not identifying with the pupil. Empathising allows the pupil to know that the teacher can understand her/his point of view while retaining a 'professional distance' (Lawrence, 1996).

As noted in Chapter 3, in order to develop such a quality relationship, the teacher needs to reflect on her/his attitude to the pupils in the class, and the way s/he interacts with them (Mosley, 1996).

Dealing with disruptive behaviour Care must be taken to ensure that the teacher's response to any inappropriate behaviour is consistent with maintaining pupil self-esteem. Thus, for example, the action of running around the classroom by a hyperactive pupil might cause the teacher's papers to be knocked over. Response 1 might be:

Teacher: 'You are silly. Why don't you take more care?'
Pupil: 'Sorry, miss.'
Teacher: 'You really are clumsy, but I suppose you'll grow out of it one day.'
Pupil: 'Sorry, miss.'

which is likely to have a deleterious effect on self-esteem. In contrast, Response 2:

Teacher: 'I get so cross when my things get knocked over.'
Pupil: 'Sorry, miss.'
Teacher: 'I need to keep my things in order, so that I find them easily.'
Pupil: 'I'll pick them up, miss.'
Teacher: 'That would be kind.'

is likely to have a neutral or even a positive effect on the pupil's self-esteem (based on Gordon, 1974).

Whereas in the first response the emphasis is on 'you', the pupil, being wrong, and on asking the pupil to explain her/his behaviour, in the second response the teacher focuses on the actions rather than on the pupil, and on how 'I', the teacher, felt about what happened.

It has also been suggested by Lawrence (1996) that, if teacher-pupil interactions are to be based on a spirit of trust, then teachers' responses should be 'genuine' and 'authentic'. The corollary of this is that if they are angry, teachers should show their anger rather than try to dissimulate, which would be inauthentic. This, however, raises the question as to how a teacher can show anger, without the anger being interpreted by pupils as a criticism of them as individuals – as distinct from being a response to something they have done. Here again, it is what is actually said that is important.

Thus, in the case of an impulsive pupil who is always interrupting when the teacher is speaking, Response 1 might be:

Teacher: 'I'm tired of silly calling out behaviour during story time'

whereas Response 2 might be:

'It is difficult for me concentrate on reading the story when there are lots of interruptions.'

The first response is a put-down, the second seeks to talk about the behaviour in a logical, cause-and-effect way, and thus maintain self-esteem.

Dealing with pupils who are tense or depressed It is sometimes the case that pupils, including those with AD/HD, feel tense and/or depressed in class, and at the idea of coming to school at all. When pupils are in such a state, their self-esteem can be very vulnerable, which means that it is important, (a) that the teacher be sensitive to how the pupil is feeling; and (b) that the teacher be particular vigilant in self-monitoring what s/he says.

In most cases, a pupil who is tense and/or depressed wants to communicate this to someone, usually the teacher or LSA, but may wish to do so at a time that is not con-venient in terms of the ongoing management of the class. This puts an additional burden on the teacher, who has not only to find appropriate words, or propose an appropriate course of action, during a one-to-one discussion with the pupil, but also to find a way of postponing the discussion to a convenient time and place. When such situations arise during a lesson, it is important that the teacher signal her/his understanding of the pupil's feelings in some way. Responses such as,

'I understand that you are feeling sad, Johnny', or
'I can see that you are feeling unhappy about this, Mary',

followed immediately by the suggestion of a time and place when the matter can be discussed in private, would be appropriate. In this way, the pupil's self-esteem is not damaged, since the teacher signals that the feelings that the pupil has are quite legitimate feelings to have. S/he also signals a positive valuation of the pupil, since s/he is willing to devote time to talking about those feelings. Most certainly, to interpret the behaviour as in any way confrontational would not only be to misinterpret the pupil's message, but might lead to the pupil receiving a mild kind of punishment, such as withdrawal of teacher gaze, with a consequent negative effect on self-esteem.

Dealing with pupils' defence mechanisms The way in which each of us behaves does not always seem rational, for example, being in a bad temper for no reason or displaying unprovoked aggression. According to Rogers (1961), such behaviours can best be interpreted as 'defence mechanisms', designed to compensate for threats to our self-esteem. Other defence mechanisms used by children and adults alike include: belittling or blaming others; boasting or inventing stories; failure to start work or school avoidance; aggressive behaviour and bullying; low motivation and 'learned helplessness', associated with fear of failure (DFE, 1994; Lawrence, 1996). All of these are found among pupils of all ages, including – but most certainly, not exclusively – those with AD/HD.

In all cases, it is important:

- to interpret the behaviour as a response from the pupil which is logical, at least from her/his point of view, rather than as a manifestation of deliberately confrontational behaviour;
- to respond to the pupil's actions in ways that are consistent with maintaining her/his self-esteem;
- to adopt the Confidence-Competence model for increasing competence and enhancing self-esteem.

Case study 3: Harriet – IEP (continued)

Principal long-term targets:
- *To increase academic attainment, by focusing on listening and communicating (initially in a small group, later in whole-class sessions), then to increase her attention span on other literacy tasks, and help her with sequencing activities in story writing;*
- *To enhance Harriet's self-esteem.*

Targets (academic):
- *To encourage Harriet to listen more carefully to the teacher during Literacy Hour;*
- *To encourage her to communicate more during small group work, starting with at least one contribution per session, during small group work, and aiming for her making contributions during the plenary session;*

Targets (interpersonal and behavioural):
Targets (self-esteem):
- *To build up Harriet's self-confidence by talking about and praising her work in art, and arranging for it to be displayed in the classroom;*

- *To build up Harriet's confidence to talk, initially in a small group, later in front of the class.*

Strategies (academic):
- *To arrange for teacher/classroom assistant to work closely with Harriet during group work and whole-class activities;*
- *To encourage her to talk to the teacher/classroom assistant about her paintings and drawings (increase communication);*
- *To remove all distracting objects from her work area.*

Strategies (interpersonal and behavioural):
- *None*

Strategies (self-esteem):
- *To warn Harriet in advance of questions, and then direct easy questions at her, during group work during Literacy Hour;*
- *To talk about the different talents that children have, during Circle Time;*
- *To encourage her to talk to the teacher/classroom assistant about her paintings and drawings (enhance self-esteem);*
- *To seek out opportunities to give Harriet private and public praise on the basis of genuine achievements.*

Monitoring and assessment:
Harriet's attainment and progress to be reviewed by class teacher, classroom assistant and SENCO each half-term.

Home-school links:
Parents to be invited to school to discuss, to plan and to arrange support language activities at home. A weekly report to be sent to the parents, using the school's pro-forma.

Strengths of the IEP include: (i) that it addresses the two areas (attainment and self-esteem) in a complementary way; (ii) that it sets out a sequence of activities designed to encourage and enable Harriet to communicate; (iii) that it does not tackle too many curriculum areas (organisation in English, with inattention and organisation in mathematics and other subjects postponed until Harriet gains a measure of self-confidence); (iv) that it does not seek to tackle too many aspects of AD/HD behaviour, e.g., fidgeting; (v) that the parents are encouraged to take an active role.

It could be improved by specifying more precisely how the parents could become involved.

CHAPTER 8

Multi-agency support

This chapter addresses three aspects of multi-agency support – the range of professionals that can support children with AD/HD, an understanding of the pros and cons of
medication and teacher stress.

Range of multi-agency support

Appropriate multi-agency support can only be achieved if individuals from the following
groups communicate and cooperate successfully with one another (BPS, 2000):

- Family and local community – parent(s)/carer(s); relatives and friends; target child;
  parent support groups; community associations.
- Education – class teacher and other teaching and learning support staff, e.g., LSA;
  SENCO; pastoral support staff; home-school liaison teacher; headteacher; educational
  psychologist and school's psychological service; behavioural support or social/educa-
  tional inclusion service; education welfare officer; LEA SEN services.
- Health – clinical psychologist; paediatrician or child psychiatrist; child psychotherapist;
  general medical practitioner; health visitor; school nurse and school medical officer;
  speech and language therapist; audiologist; dietician.
- Social services – social worker; probation officer or youth justice officer; police.

The particular roles that each of the professional groups fulfil have been described by
Farrell (2000). In many local authorities clearly defined policies and practice have been
established and multi-disciplinary teams have been formed that work effectively together
(e.g., BPS, 2000; Holowencko, 1999).

Ideally, those individuals involved in undertaking an assessment, or planning an intervention programme, hold a case conference to exchange information based on their different
perspectives. In other cases, information has to be communicated through written reports.

Pros and cons of medical intervention

The use of medication for treating AD/HD is the subject of much research and discussion. At one extreme is the view that such medication should not be prescribed, on the grounds that there is no evidence that AD/HD is caused by a biological brain dysfunction, that there are no scientific criteria for AD/HD and that methylphenidate is 'a core member of the family of amphetamines' (Baldwin, 2000: 598), which have the potential for abuse and addiction. The alternative argument is that for many children the educational and social advantages of medication outweigh disadvantages, provided that certain precautions are taken. These are: (i) that medication should only be prescribed following a detailed diagnosis, undertaken by a specialist medical practitioner; (ii) that, when prescribed, the effect of drugs should be monitored carefully for any side-effects; and (iii) that periods of 'drug vacation' should be planned, so that the necessity of continuing the medication can be determined (Cooper, 2000; Doherty, *et al.*, 2000; Frankenberger and Cannon, 1999; Hinshaw, *et al.*, 1998; Kewley, 1999a and b; NICE, 2000; Wright, 1997).

Arguments in favour of medication

Medication seeks to treat the core symptoms of inattention, hyperactivity and impulsiveness by correcting a brain dysfunction, and thus increase educational attainment, interpersonal relations and self-esteem by improving behaviours such as distractibility, concentration, oppositionality and aggression and also working memory. It can be seen to provide a '*window of opportunity*' for the child to benefit from teaching-learning experiences provided by teachers, parents and others. It is certainly the case that the hyperactive and impulsive behaviour in class and at home of many children is significantly reduced when they are on the correct dosage of an appropriate medication. This can have beneficial effects on their own learning and on relationships within the classroom and at home.

Some studies, including a meta-analysis of 135 studies which suggested an average increase of 15 percentile points, indicate beneficial effects of Ritalin on academic attainment, in line with what would be predicted. Improvements were also reported in social interactions and peer relationships. These findings have not, however, always been confirmed by other studies. Reasons for such discrepancies may be attributable to failure to control for the type and severity of the AD/HD, and/or for type and dosage of medication, and/or for the existence of other associated or co-morbid conditions, and/or the type and quality of the accompanying educational intervention, if any. Certainly, the studies have been of short duration, from six months to four or five years.

Proponents of the use of medication argue that it should be used as early as the symptoms appear, so as to prevent educational and social failure, rather than as a last resort, or suitable for only the most severe cases. At the same time, it is cautioned that such medication should not be regarded as bringing about a 'cure', but rather as controlling a dysfunction, as with asthma or diabetes, and some drugs work more effectively than others for different children. Experienced AD/HD clinics report improvement in symptoms in 80 to 95 per cent of cases (Kewley, 1999a), while 85 per cent of children reported that they wished to continue taking Ritalin (Doherty, *et al.*, 2000). NICE (2000) has presented evidence which suggests that the addition of medication to behavioural treatment programmes is beneficial, at least in short-and medium-term outcomes.

Arguments against using medication

The principal arguments are: (i) that it may have side-effects; (ii) that it may be addictive; and (iii) that long-term efficacy has not been evaluated. Reported side-effects include: appetite suppression (or the reverse); abdominal pain/headaches, which may be secondary effects of stress and rarely persist; loss of sparkle; sleep difficulties; rebound effects, such that hyperactivity increases as the effects of the drug wear off; tics, which may be related to Tourette Syndrome (Carroll and Robinson, 2000) but may be controlled by additional medication; other side-effects, such as itchy skin or mood change; and growth, though this tends to relate to timing rather than final height. Of these, sleep difficulties, particularly with deep or 'REM' sleep, is perhaps of most concern to teachers, since it affects learning, and young children characteristically spend a lot of time in REM sleep. There is no evidence of addiction to, or substance abuse of, stimulants used in the treatment of AD/HD (see Kewley (1999a) for further discussion).

Medical, educational and combined treatments

Some children with AD/HD can benefit from educational/behavioural intervention alone. However, where medication is prescribed, its effect is significantly greater in combination with appropriate educational or behaviour provision. In terms of academic attainment, even by the time of diagnosis, a child is likely to have developed complex learning difficulties, consequent upon her/his problems with attending to and processing information. Similar difficulties are likely to arise, even from earliest age, with interpersonal relations. For many children, ideal provision would include intensive support from teachers, psychologists, family therapists and others (Braswell and Bloomquist, 1991; Teeter, 1998).

Teacher stress

The keys to dealing with teacher stress are: Confidence and Competence. Ways in which teachers can increase their competence in teaching children with AD/HD have been discussed in the previous chapters and are touched on here. The issue of confidence is more complicated because it is so intimately related to our self-concept – what it means to be me. Paradoxically, the first stage in increasing confidence is to have the confidence to admit that you are stressed. One of the most common symptoms of extreme stress is denial that anything is wrong. Such a denial is often based on the belief that to admit you are stressed is, in some way, to accuse yourself of failing. Fortunately, we now live in a society in which job-related stress is a commonly accepted phenomenon to which a stigma is no longer attached – unfortunately, of course, job related stress has come to be a fact of life for many people.

Admitting that you are stressed

Thus, stage 1 in increasing self-confidence is, either in discussion with a partner or trusted colleague, to admit that certain aspects of teaching in your class and/or at your school is causing you to be stressed. Interestingly, you may find that you are not alone in the staff room, in which case how to deal with stress may become a departmental or whole school issue.

Teachers' self-esteem

Stage 2, is to find ways of increasing self-confidence. As every teacher knows, teaching is an inherently demanding job. It is also a job which can be the source of considerable job satisfaction. However, such satisfaction can be reduced significantly as a result of having to cope with a difficult class. Furthermore, lack of job satisfaction can lead to low self-esteem and to stress.

The key to dealing with this kind of situation is summarised in the 'IRIAM Model of Staff Development'. An example of the way in which the model can be used to analyse and promote successful action is as follows:

Identify those aspects of your teaching that are causing you concern,
e.g., *the teacher identified disruptive behaviour as the area for concern.*

Reflect upon the nature of your anxieties and concerns and how they impinge on your teaching in general – you will find it useful to discuss these with colleagues in the staff room, since it is likely that your anxieties and concerns will be experienced by others, *e.g., the teacher thought carefully about all the ways in which the disruptive behaviour affected her teaching in the classroom, and the effect on the other pupils' learning and behaviour. This was done together with two experienced and respected colleagues, and led to a more precise formulation of the problem.*

Inform yourself about ways of dealing with situations that you find it difficult to handle – this can be done by reading or by attending an INSET course, or as a result of a focused discussion and brainstorming session with colleagues,

e.g., having formulated the problem more precisely, the teacher sought advice from other colleagues and from the school's educational psychologist. The educational psychologist organised an INSET event for the whole staff, at which they focused their attention on:

(a) describing in detail the child's behaviour and the responses of the teacher, learning support assistant and other pupils;

(b) describing in detail the behaviour of other disruptive pupils that different members of staff had taught in the past;

(c) describing in detail the strategies and techniques that they had employed in the past and the extent to which they were effective;

(d) analysing the different strategies and techniques used to determine any common principles or themes, and the extent to which the strategies and techniques were effective.

In this way, the staff were able to identify expertise which they already possessed that could be used in this new situation. The educational psychologist informed the staff about ways in which a pupil with AD/HD may differ from other pupils with EBD, for example, the way they respond to different kinds of reinforcements, and the staff formulated a whole-school plan.

Act on the basis of the information you have gained – try out some of the ideas that you have read about or discussed,

e.g., baseline data were collected and recorded of the target pupil's behaviour, and teacher and fellow pupil responses. A number of specific criteria were proposed to determine whether or not the plan could be judged to be effective. Some of these criteria related to amount of on-task academic activities, some to behaviour in the classroom, some to behaviour at lunchtime and in the playground. The plan was implemented, initially over a four-week period.

Monitor the extent to which these different ideas are effective – in doing so, you will first need to establish a 'baseline' of what classroom interactions were like before you introduced new or modified methods,

e.g., the effectiveness of the plan, including the effectiveness of the teachers' action, were assessed at the end of the four-week period, and the plan was modified slightly in the light of experience (based, in part, on Johnson, 2000).

The postscript to this intervention is, (i) that the approach was judged to be effective after three months, and (ii) that the teacher maintained self-esteem.

To the future

It is undoubtedly the case that children with AD/HD can be extremely challenging; it is also true both that they can be very rewarding to teach and that many subsequently become respected individuals with important professional and managerial responsibilities. The challenge to teachers and others is to find ways that their undoubted qualities can first be understood and then developed and fostered.

Where to find help and advice

Action Against Allergy
PO Box 278
Twickenham, Middlesex, TW1 4QQ
Tel: 020 892 2711

ADDISS – ADD Information Services
PO Box 340
Edgware, Middlesex, HA8 9HL
Tel: 020 8906 9088
Fax: 020 8959 0727
www.addiss.co.uk
e-mail: Info@addiss.co.uk

ADD/ADHD Support Group (London)
88 Penshurst Gardens
Edgware, Middlesex, HA8 9TU
Tel: 020 8958 6727

ADD-ADHD Family Support Group
1a High Street
Dilton Marsh
Westbury, Wiltshire, SN10 1PT
Tel: 01373 826045

and

93 Avon Road
Devizes, Wiltshire, SN10 1PT
Tel: 01380 726 710
www.pncl.co.uk/prosper/adhd.html

ADDnet UK
10 Troughton Road
Charlton, London SE7 7QH
Tel/fax: 020 8305 1023
www.web-tv.co.uk/addnet.html

Afasic
69–85 Old Street
London, EC1V 9HX
Tel: 020 7841 8900

Association of Workers for Children with
Emotional Behaviour
Difficulties (AWCEBD)
20 Carlton Street
Kettering, Northants., NN16 8EB
Tel/fax: 01536 5518455

British Dyslexia Association
National Organisation for Specific Learning
Difficulties
98 London Road
Reading, Berkshire, RG1 5AU
Tel: 01734 662677
Fax: 01734 351927

British Society for Allergy, Environmental
and Nutritional Medicine (BSAENM)
PO Box 7
Knighton, LD7 1WF

Canadian Association for Children with
Learning Difficulties
Kildare House
323 Chapel Street
Ottawa
Ontario, KIN 7Z2
Tel: +1 (603) 238-5721

Children and Adults with Attention Deficit
Disorders (CHADD)
1859 North Pine Island Road, Suite 185
Plantation, FL 33322 USA
Tel: +1 (305) 587 3700
www.chadd.org

Hyperactive Children's Support Group
(HACSG)
71 Whyke Lane
Chichester, West Sussex, PO19 2LD
Tel: 01903 725182

LADDER
National Learning and Attention Deficit
Disorders Association
142 Mostyn Road
London, SW19 3LR

or

95 Church Road
Bradmore
Wolverhampton, WV3 7EW

Learning Assessment Centre
2nd floor, 44 Springfield Road,
Horsham, West Sussex, RH12 2PD
Tel: 01403 240002
Fax: 01403 260900

The Mental Health Foundation
37 Mortimer Street
London, W1N 8JU
Tel: 020 7580 0145
Fax: 020 7631 3868

NICE
National Institute for Clinical Excellence
Tel: 0541 555 455, quoting reference 22593
www.nice.og.uk

The Tavistock and Portman NHS Trust
Child and Family Department
Tavistock Clinic
120 Belsize Lane
London, NW3 5BA
Tel: 020 7435 7111

Tourette Syndrome Associates
42-40 Bell Boulevard
Bayside, New York 10016 US
Tel: +1 (718) 224 2999

University of Massachusetts
Department of Psychiatry
University of Massachusetts Medical Center
Attention Deficit Hyperactivity Disorder
Clinic
55 Lake Avenue North
Worcester, MA 01655-0239 USA
Tel: +1 (508) 8956-2552
Fax: +1 (508) 856-3595

Other websites:

www.pavillion.co.uk/add/english.html
www.patient.org.uk
www.azstarnet.com/~ask
www.ncet.org.uk/senco
www.add.org
www.shef.ac.uk/~psyc/InterPsych/inter.html
www.mediconsult.com/frames/add
www.aacap.org

References

Ainscow, M. (1997) 'Towards inclusive schooling', *British Journal of Special Education* **24**, 3–6.

Alban-Metcalfe, J. (1998) 'School failure in the United Kingdom' *European Journal of Teacher Education* **21**, 367–95.

Alban-Metcalfe, J. *et al.* (2001) 'Teacher and student teacher ratings of Attention-Deficit/Hyperactivity Disorder', (submitted for publication).

Alban-Metcalfe, S. Juliette (1999) 'Attention-Deficit/Hyperactivity disorder symptoms among undergraduates and their relationship with learning style'. Unpublished BSc dissertation. University of London, Goldsmiths College, Department of Psychology.

Alimo-Metcalfe, B. and Alban-Metcalfe, R. J. (2001) 'The development of a new transformational leadership questionnaire', *Journal of Occupational and Organizational Psychology* **74**, 1–28.

American Psychiatric Association (2000) Diagnostic and Statistical Manual of Mental Disorders, 4th edn. text revision – (DSM-IV-TR). Washington, DC: American Psychiatric Association.

Armstrong, D. (1995) *Power and Partnership: Parents, children and special educational needs.* London: Routledge.

Asarnow, J. R. and Callan, J. W. (1985) 'Boys with peer adjustment problems: social cognitive processes', *Journal of Consulting and Clinical Psychology* **53**, 80–87.

Ayllon, T. *et al.* (1975) 'A behavioural-educational alternative to drug control of hyperactive children', *Journal of Applied Behavior Analysis* **8**, 137–46.

Baldwin, S. (2000) 'How should ADHD be treated?', *The Psychologist* **13**, 598–602.

Barkley, R. A. (1989) 'Attention-Deficit Hyperactivity Disorder'. in Mash, E. J. and Barkley, R. A. (eds) *Treatment of Childhood Disorders*, 39–72. New York: Guilford.

Barkley, R. A. (1997) *ADHD and the Nature of Self-control.* New York: Guilford.

Barkley, R. A. (1998) *Attention-Deficit Hyperactivity Disorder: A handbook for diagnosis and treatment.* 2nd edn. New York: Guilford.

Beelmann, A. *et al.* (1994) 'Effects of training social competence in children: a meta-analysis of recent evaluation studies', *Journal of Abnormal Child Psychology* **5**, 265–75.

Bennathan, M. and Boxall, M. (1997) *Effective Intervention in Primary Schools: Nurture groups.* London: David Fulton Publishers.

Bennett, N. *et al.* (1997) 'Teaching through play: teachers' thinking and classroom practice'. Buckingham: Open University.

Blamires, M. *et al.* (1997) *Parent-teacher Partnership: Practical approaches to meet special educational needs.* London: David Fulton Publishers.

Boud, D. and Feletti, G. (ed.) (1997) *The Challenge of Problem-based Learning*, 2nd edn. London: Kogan Page.

BPS (British Psychological Society) (1996) *Attention-Deficit/Hyperactivity Disorder: A psychological response to an evolving concept.* Leicester: British Psychological Society.

BPS (2000) *Attention-Deficit/Hyperactivity Disorder: Guidelines and principles for successful multi-agency working*. Leicester: British Psychological Society.

Braswell, L. and Bloomquist, M. L. (1991) *Cognitive-behavior Therapy with ADHD Children: Child, family, and school interventions*. New York: Guilford.

Brown, T. (1995) 'Differential diagnosis of ADD versus ADHD in adults', in Nadeau K. G. (ed.) *A Comprehensive Guide to Attention Deficit Disorder in Adults: Research, diagnosis and treatment*, 93–108. New York: Brunner/Mazel.

Bullock, K. and Wikeley, F. (1999) 'Improving learning in Year 9: making use of personal learning plans' *Educational Studies* **25**, 19–33.

Burns, R. B. (1982) *Self-concept Development and Academic Attainment*. London: Holt.

Cantwell, D. P. and Baler, L. (1991) 'Association between attention-deficit hyperactivity disorder and learning disorders', *Journal of Learning Disorders* **24**, 88–95.

Carlson, C. (1997) *Assessment and Nonpharmocological Treatment of ADHD*. Research abstract presented at the annual meeting of CH.A.D.D., San Antonio, TX, cited by Teeter (1998).

Carroll, A. and Robinson, A. (2000) *Tourette Syndrome: A practical guide for teachers, parents and carers*. London: David Fulton Publishers.

Cooley, C. H. (1902) *Human Nature and the Social Order*. New York: Charles Scriber's Sons.

Cooper, P. (1999) 'Making sense of ADHD', in Cooper, P. and Bilton, K. (eds) *ADHD: Research, Practice and Opinion*. London: Whurr.

Cooper, P. (2000) 'How should ADHD be treated?', *The Psychologist* **13**, 598–602.

Cooper, P. and Ideus, K. (1996) *Attention Deficit/Hyperactivity Disorder: A practical guide for teachers*. London: David Fulton Publishers.

Croll, P. & Moses, P. (2000) *Special Needs in the Primary School: One in five?* London: Cassell.

Department of Education (1993) *Report of the Special Education Review Committee*. Dublin, Eire: Department of Education.

Department of Education for Northern Ireland (1998) *The Code of Practice for the Identification and Assessment of Special Educational Needs*. HMSO: Belfast.

DES (Department of Education and Science) (1978) *Special Educational Needs*. (The Warnock Report.) London: HMSO.

DES (1989) *Aspects of Primary Education: The education of children under five*. London: HMSO.

DES (1990) *Starting with Quality: Report of the committee of enquiry into quality educational experiences offered to 3- to 4-year-olds*. London: HMSO.

DFE (1994) *The Education of Children with Emotional and Behavioural Difficulties (Circular 9/94)*. London: DFE.

DfEE (Department for Education and Employment) (1999) *Research Report: Provision for pupils with emotional and behavioural difficulties in mainstream schools*. London: DfEE.

DfEE (2000a) *The SEN Code of Practice (Draft Version)*. London: DfEE

DfEE (2000b) *The National Literacy Strategy: Supporting pupils with special educational needs in the literacy hour*. London: DfEE.

DfEE/QCA (1999). *National Curriculum for England: Citizenship*. London: DfEE/QCA

Dodge, K. A. and Price, J. M. (1994) 'On the relation between social information processing and socially competent behaviour in early school-aged children', *Child Development* **65**, 1385–97.

Doherty, S. L., *et al.* (2000) 'Children's self-reported effects of stimulant medication', *International Journal of Disability, Development and Education* **47**, 39–54.

Drayton, M. (1999) 'The role and purpose of school governing bodies', in Cole, M. (ed.) *Professional Issues for Teachers and Student Teachers*, 95–109. London: David Fulton Publishers.

DuPaul, G. J. and Stoner, G. (1994) *ADHD and the Schools: Assessment and intervention strategies*. New York: Guilford.

Education Act (1998) Dublin, Eire.

Elias, M. J. and Clabby, J. F. (1989) *Social Decision Making Skills: A curriculum guide for elementary grades.* Gaitherburg, MD: Aspen.

Everett, C. A. and Everett, S. V. (2000) *Family Therapy for ADHD: Treating children, adolescents, and adults.* New York: Guilford.

Farrell, M. (1998) 'Notes on the green paper: an initial response', *British Journal of Special Education* **25**, 13–15

Farrell, M. (2000) *The Special Education Handbook,* 2nd edn. London: David Fulton Publishers.

Fisher, R. (ed.) (1987) *Problem-solving in Primary Schools.* Oxford: Blackwell.

Fletcher, J. (1999) *Marching to a Different Tune: Diary about an ADHD boy.* London: Jessica Kingsley.

Fowler, M. (1992) *CH.A.D.D. Educator's Manual; An in-depth look at attention-deficit disorders from an educational perspective.* Fairfax, VA: CASET.

Frank, J. (1999) 'Struggles with an inebriated horse: The pain of having ADHD', in Cooper, P. and Bilton, K. (eds) *ADHD: Research, Practice and Opinion,* 33–9. London: Whurr.

Frankenberger, W. and Cannon, C. (1999) 'Effects of Ritalin on academic achievement from first to fifth grade', *International Journal of Disability, Development and Education* **46**, 199–221.

Goldstein, S. and Goldstein, N. (1990) *Managing Attention Disorders in Children.* New York: Wiley-Interscience.

Gordon, T. (1974) *Teacher Effectiveness Training.* New York: Peter H. Wyden.

Green, R. W. (1995) 'Students with ADHD in school classrooms: teacher factors related to compatibility, assessment and intervention', *School Psychology Review* **24**, 81–93

Hanko, G. (1999) *Increasing Competence through Collaborative Problem-solving: Using insights into social and emotional factors in children's learning.* London: David Fulton Publishers

Harris, J. *et al.* (1997) *Pupils with Severe Learning Disabilities who Present Challenging Behaviour.* Kidderminster: BILD.

Harter, S. and Pike, P. (1984) 'The pictorial perceived competence scale for young children', *Child Education* **55**, 1969–82.

Hinshaw, S. P. *et al.* (1998) 'Childhood attention deficit hyperactivity disorder: nonpharmocological and combination treatments', in Nathan, P. and Gorman, M. (eds) *A Guide to Treatments that Work,* 26–41. Oxford: Oxford University Press.

Holowenko, H. (1999) *Attention Deficit/Hyperactivity Disorder: A multidisciplinary approach.* London: Jessica Kingsley.

Hughes, F. P. (1991) *Children, Play and Development.* Needham Heights, MA: Allyn & Bacon.

Hutt, S. J. *et al.* (1989) *Play, Exploration and Learning.* London: Routledge.

Johnson, C. (2000) Personal communication.

Kewley, G. (1999a) *ADHD – Recognition, Reality and Resolution.* Horsham, Surrey: LAC Press.

Kewley, G. (1999b) 'The role of medication in a multi-modal approach to the management of ADHD', in Cooper, P. and Bilton, K. (eds) *ADHD: Research, Practice and Opinion,* 60–75. London: Whurr.

Kinder, J. (1999) 'ADHD – A different viewpoint I: dietary factors', in Cooper, P. and Bilton, K. (eds) *ADHD: Research, Practice and Opinion,* 76–110. London: Whurr.

Laslett, R. (1982) *Maladjusted Children in the Ordinary School.* Stratford-upon-Avon: National Council for Special Education.

Lawrence, D. (1996) *Enhancing Self-esteem in the Classroom,* 2nd Edn. London: Paul Chapman.

Letch, R. (2000) 'Special educational needs and inclusion', in Dockling, J. (ed.) *New Labour's Policies for Schools: Raising the standards?* 105–18. London: David Fulton Publishers.

Lewis, A. (1992) 'From planning to practice' *British Journal of Special Education* **19**, 24–7.

Lindsley, O. R. (1991) 'From technical jargon to plain English for application', *Journal of Applied Behavioral Analysis* **24**, (1), 449–58

Lorenz, S. (2001) *First Steps in Inclusion: A handbook for teachers, school governors and managers, and LEAs.* London: David Fulton Publishers.

Markel, G. and Greenbaum, J. (1996) *Performance Breakthroughs for Adolescents with Learning Disabilities or ADD.* Champaign, IL: Research Press.

Meadows, S. and Cashdan, A. (1988) *Helping Children Learn.* London: David Fulton Publishers.

Mercer, C. D. and Mercer, A. R. (1993) *Teaching Students with Learning Problems*, 4th edn. Columbus OH: Merrill.

Mittler, P. (2000) *Working Towards Inclusive Education: Social Contexts.* London: David Fulton Publishers

Molina y Garcia, S. and Alban-Metcalfe, J. (1998) 'Integrated or inclusive education versus interactive education: the need for a new model', *European Journal of Special Needs Education* **13**, 170–79.

Monighan-Nourot, P. *et al.* (1987) *Looking at Children's Play: A bridge between theory and practice.* New York: Teachers College Press.

Mosley, J. (1996) *Quality Circle Time in the Primary Classroom.* vol. 1. Cambridge: LDA.

Mosley, J. (1998) *More Quality Circle Time in the Primary Classroom.* vol. 2. Cambridge: LDA.

Mosley, J. (1999) *Quality Circle Time in the Secondary School.* London: David Fulton Publishers.

Munden, A. and Arcelus, J. (1999) *The ADHD Handbook: A guide for parents and professionals.* Birmingham: Birmingham Children's Hospital Trust.

NICE (National Institute for Clinical Excellence) (2000) Guidance for the Use of Methylphenidate for ADHD. London: National Institute for Clinical Excellence.

OFSTED (1999) *Principles into Practice: Effective Education for Pupils with Emotional and Behavioural Difficulties.* London: OFSTED.

OFSTED (2000) *Strategies to Promote Educational Inclusion: Improving city schools.* London: OFSTED.

OFSTED (undated) *Evaluating Educational Inclusion: Guidance for inspectors and schools.* London: OFSTED.

Pfiffer, L. J. and Barkley, R. A. (1990) 'Educational placement and classroom management' in Barkley, R. A. *Attention-deficit Hyperactivity Disorder: A handbook for diagnosis and treatment*, 498–539. New York: Guilford.

Pliszka, S. R. *et al.* (1999) *ADHD with Cormorbid Disorders: Clinical assessment and management.* New York: Guilford.

Portwood, M. (2000) *Understanding Developmental Dyspraxia: A textbook for students and professionals*, 2nd edn. London: David Fulton Publishers.

Poulou, M. and Norwich, B. (2000) 'Teachers' causal attributions, cognitive, emotional and behavioural responses to students with emotional and behavioural difficulties', *British Journal of Educational Psychology* **70**, 559–81.

Report of the Special Education Review Committee (1993) Dublin: Stationery Office.

Reid, R. and Maag, J. W. (1994) 'How many "fidgets" in a "pretty much": A critique of behaviour rating scales for identifying children with ADHD', *Journal of School Psychology* **32**, 339–54

Reif, S. (1993) *How to Reach and Teach ADD/ADHD Children.* West Nyack, NY: Center for Applied Research in Education.

Richards, I. C. (1999) 'Inclusive schools for pupils with emotional and behavioural difficulties', *Support for Learning* **14**, 99–103.

Robin, A. L. (1998) *ADHD in Adolescents: Diagnosis and treatment.* New York: Guilford.

Robbins, B. (2000) *Inclusive Mathematics 5–11.* London: Continuum.

Rogers, C. R. (1961) *On Becoming a Person.* Boston, MA: Houghton-Mifflin.

SED (Scottish Education Department) (1978) *Progress Report: The education of pupils with learning difficulties in primary and secondary schools in Scotland.* Edinburgh: HMSO.

Scottish Office (1994) *Effective Provision for Special Educational Needs*. Edinburgh: HMSO.

Scottish Office (1996) *Children and Young Persons with Special Educational Needs: Assessment and recording*. Edinburgh: HMSO.

Shapiro, E. S. and Cole, C. L. (1994) *Behavior Change in the Classroom: Self-management interventions*. New York: Guilford.

Shelton, T. (1992) 'UMASS kindergarten behavior management programme'. Unpublished ms, cited by Teeter (1998).

Shure, M. B. (1983) 'Enhancing childrearing skills in lower income women', *Issues in Mental Health Nursing* 5 (1–4), 121–38.

Shure, M. B. (1994) *I Can Problem Solve (ICPS): An interpersonal cognitive problem-solving program for children*. Champaign, Il; Research Press.

Smilansky, S. (1990) 'Socio-dramatic play: its relevance to behaviour and achievement in school', in Klugman, E. and Smilansky, S. (eds) *Child's Play and Learning Perspectives and Policy Implications*. New York: Teacher's College Press.

Smith, D. J. *et al.* (1992). 'The effect of a self-management procedure on the classroom academic behavior of students with mild handicaps', School Psychological Review 21, 59–72.

Sonuga-Barke, E. J. S. and Goldfoot, M. (1995) 'The effect of childhood hyperactivity on mothers' expectations for development', *Child: Care, Health and Development* 21, 17–39

Sonuga-Barke, E. J. S. *et al.* (1993) 'Inter-ethnic bias in teachers' ratings of childhood hyperactivity', *British Journal of Developmental Psychology* 11, 187–200.

Still, G. F. (1902) 'Some abnormal psychical conditions in children', Lancet, i, 1008–12, 1077–83, 1163–68.

Stokes, T. F. and Osnes, P. G. (1989) 'An operant pursuit generalization', *Behavior Therapy* 20, 337–55.

Sweeney, D. (1999) 'Liaising with parents, carers and agencies' in Cole, M. (ed.) *Professional Issues for Teachers and Student Teachers*, 85–94. London: David Fulton Publishers.

Sylva, K., *et al.* (1980) *Childwatching at Playgroup and Nursery*. London: Grant McIntyre.

Tannock, R. (1998) 'ADHD: Advances in cognitive, neurobiological and genetic research', *Journal of Child Psychology and Psychiatry* 37, 65–99.

Teeter, P. A. (1998) *Interventions for ADHD: Treatment in Developmental Context*. New York: Guilford.

Teeter, P. A. and Stewart, P. (1997) *ADD and Problem-solving Communication: A model for home-school-physician partnership*. Madison, WI: Wisconsin Department of Public Instruction Report.

Vygotsky, L. (1978) *Mind in Society: The development of higher psychological processes*. Cambridge, MA: MIT Press.

Weaver, C. (ed.) (1994) *Success at Last: Helping students with AD(H)D achieve their potential*. Portsmouth, NH: Henemann.

Webster-Stratton, C. (1999) *How to Promote Children's Social and Emotional Competence*. London: Paul Chapman.

Webster-Stratton, C. and Hammond, M. (1997) 'Treating children with early-onset conduct problems: a comparison of child and parent training interventions', *Journal of Consulting and Clinical Psychology* 65: 1, 93–109

Wood, E. and Attfield, J. (1996) *Play, Learning and the Early Childhood Curriculum*. London: Paul Chapman.

WHO (World Health Organization) (1990) *International Classification of Diseases – 10 (ICD – 10)*. Geneva: World Health Organization.

Wright, S. (1997) '"A little understood solution to a vaguely defined problem": parental perceptions of Ritalin', *Education and Child Psychology* 41, 50–59.

Index